MW00412442

From the News to the Pews

Warm-Hearted Stories of Family, Faith, Laughter, and Love

by

Steve Davis

To Karen,
Enjoy the book.
Love,
Steve

VA

Vabella Publishing
P.O. Box 1052
Carrollton, Georgia 30112
www.vabella.com

Copyright © 2013 by Steve Davis

All rights reserved. No part of the book may be reproduced or utilized in any form or by any means without permission in writing from the author. All requests should be addressed to the publisher.

Cover design by Susan Mashburn

Manufactured in the United States of America

Library of Congress Control Number: 2013952294

13-digit ISBN 978-1-938230-55-4

10 9 8 7 6 5 4 3 2 1

To Sheri, Tyler, and Natalie

Table of Contents

Church News

Discipleship News

Family News

Index

Preface

To my millions of imaginary fans, I say "thanks." To my handful of actual fans, I say, "What are you thinking?" I am flattered that anyone would find inspiration or humor in my writings; I humbly say that I am grateful.

A local restaurant that the Davis family visits is 302 South Street. Their sign out front says, "302: World famous in small circles." That's me—very small circles.

All of the stories in this book have appeared in our church newsletter, so I owe a lot to Susan Mashburn, my secretary and our office manager. Our church members read them to appease my ego. I'm also grateful to photographer Melanie Brooks and the many coerced parishioners who posed for the pictures on the cover. Posed? Actually, they bring newspapers to church every Sunday. Friend John Bell has published all of my books, and for that I am grateful.

These same articles have all made their way into our local newspaper, The Times-Georgian, where my faithful readers gather around one table at a local coffee shop. This exposure would not have been possible without the support of the Publisher of our paper, my friend, Leonard Woolsey.

Since the subject of some of the articles is my family, I owe an apology to Sheri, Tyler, and Natalie. They are good sports, and if I will quit subjecting them to public humiliation they have said that they will keep me around for a few more years.

So, thanks for buying a book. Thanks for buying thousands of them. One, thousands, what's the difference? Like most ministers, I am not good at math. The old joke is that my calling into ministry happened in the middle of a math class. I looked up at the heavens and asked, "Is that other job still available?" So, I became a minister and a writer and not a mathematician. Thanks for buying one. We ministers always round up. Thanks for buying thousands.

Steve Davis

Church News

From the News to the Pews

I long for its arrival. I've been known to brave the elements in my pajamas to retrieve it early in the morning. Having it in hand, and a cup of coffee, my day is off to a good start. I inherited a love of newspapers from my Dad, and now I have passed it on to our son, Tyler. I devour the sports section and read much of the rest. The daily newspaper is a welcome and honored guest in my home. It is eagerly awaited and joyously received. My attention is fixed on it, and for a little while, it is the center of my universe. And by the way, my newspaper boy could pitch for the Braves. He throws the paper in the same place every day—under my car.

But just as quickly it loses its value. Once the newspaper has been read it ceases to have value to me. Its news is no longer news. It has lost its capacity to excite me. From a pinnacle of prominence, it, much like Humpty Dumpty, takes a mighty fall. Having used it, I now abuse it. It might be used to line the cage of Polly the Parrot or be used to house break Fido. Once a treasure, it is now trash. "Honey, will you bag the newspapers?"

But alas, in our modern world, there is a thing called recycling and what was once only garbage for the dump, now can be redeemed from the dump heap. There is the possibility of rebirth for trees. And so the "good news" from the world of newspapers (you knew I would find a sermon in this) is that, in Christ, reconciliation and redemption are possible. As Paul says, "those in Christ are new creations. The old has passed away. Everything has become new" (2 Corinthians 5:17).

A well-known speaker started off his seminar by holding up a $20 bill. In a room of 200 he asked, "Who would like this $20 bill?" Hands started going up. He said, "I'm going to give this $20 bill to one of you, but let me first do this." He proceeded to crumple the bill up. He then asked, "Who still wants it?" Hands went up in the air. "Well, what if I do this?" He then dropped it and began to grind it into the floor with his shoe. He picked it up, now crumpled and dirty. "Now who wants it?" Still hands went into the air. "My friends you have learned a valuable lesson today. No matter what I did to the money, you wanted it because it did not decrease in value. It was still worth $20."

"Many times in our lives," he continued, "we are dropped, crumpled, and grounded in the dirt by the decisions we have made or the circumstances that come our way. We feel worthless. But no matter what happens, you will never lose your value to God."

So, what are you worth? Have people in your life put you down and cast doubt about your value? The scriptures remind us that we are all "made in the image of God" (Genesis 1:27-28). That alone gives each of us great value.

I'll see you at church or at the newsstand.

Dr. Phil

Nine-year-old Cole has a way of saying funny things. I think he gets that from his grandmother, Julia. Anyway, I walked into Longhorn Steakhouse for lunch with some friends, and I saw Cole sitting with his mom and dad, Chris and Melanie. Cole pointed at me and said to his folks, "There's Dr. Phil." I guess it could have been worse, like Dr. Ruth or Dr. Laura. At least he got the Dr. right.

Speaking of doctors, I was always a good student, though my senior year of college was two of the best years of my life. I crammed four years of college into five. I was having too much fun playing intramurals, and just playing, to graduate on time. I did, however, spend seven hard years in seminary obtaining two advanced degrees. So, yes, I earned a doctorate, but I could care less if you call me Dr. or Reverend. Truthfully, "Pastor Steve" has always been my favorite title from kids. I like that a tad better than Dr. Phil. Pastor describes my calling and Steve makes it personal.

Having worked hard for my educational degrees, I read with much interest a few years ago that 11 Georgia educators had their licenses revoked by the Professional Standards Commission. All 11, 10 teachers and a principal, bought advanced degrees from a university that requires little or no course work. Shame on them. That is an affront to all other educators who put in long, tough years for their professional training.

I have noticed that many preacher types like being called "Doctor," when, truthfully, some have never attended seminary and have no advanced degree work. I've known some ministerial "Doctors" who have mail-order degrees.

Why? Why do they do it, and why do churches hire them? Perhaps some ministers like to hide their insecurities with a title. Lots of folk hide behind badges and titles. Is it possible that churches might want their egos stroked by having a "doctor" in the pulpit? Who knows? It's an odd thing to say the least. I am disheartened, however, when the state Department of Education seems to have more ethics than those who profess faith in Christ. We shouldn't allow ministers with bogus, mail-order degrees to preach in our pulpits any more than schools should allow such teachers to teach.

The fact that I am writing this article points out the log in my own eye: arrogance. Those of us with earned doctorates can be awfully snooty towards those who have bogus ones. Which is worse, an earned degree with pride or a bogus one with humility? Woe is me! Paul reminded us in Romans 12:3, "I say to everyone among you not to think of yourself more highly than you ought to think."

We all know that Jesus chose a towel for service over a title for recognition. Dr. Jesus? No way.

Sincerely,

The Most Holy Father Right Reverend Doctor Steve[1]

Herniated Heart

I can tell you that not all surgeries are the same. I had cervical disc surgery a few years ago to repair a herniated disc. Before that I had knee surgery and had very little angst about it. But this disc repair was different. I was a tad worried and had a bit of fear knowing that my surgeon, Dr. Prybis, would be cutting on my neck and not my knee.

Upon arriving at Tanner Hospital, I was greeted by some smiling volunteers at the front desk. When taken to the surgical area, the first nurse I saw was Ashley, who just happens to attend our church. Her smiling face put me more at ease. Then one of my surgical nurses came in, and lo and behold, it was Michelle. She is a member of our church, and she is the kind of person who could have made Job laugh. She makes Leno, Letterman, and Chris Rock seem boring. She had me laughing, causing the pain to move from my neck to my side.

Then some caring church members came by and with them was preacher friend Jimmy, who said a prayer for me. I guess his prayer put me to sleep, along with some feel-good medicine, because the next thing I remember is waking up in a room and meeting nurse, Matissha. She was kind, patient, and professional.

---

[1] Randall O'Brien, *I Feel Better All Over Than I Do Anywhere Else* (Macon: Peake Road, 1996) 39.

I went home that evening, took off the protective neck collar and looked at my bandage in the mirror. LOL. Michelle, the surgical nurse, had left me a message on my bandage. I guess it is sort of like putting your name in newly laid concrete or carving your initials in a tree trunk. Her message to me in black marker on the neck bandage was: "Tanner (hospital) and Jesus love me."

That got me to thinking about the role of churches and hospitals. Hospitals don't typically talk about loving patients. They will speak of caring about their patients, which Tanner Medical Center does very well, by the way. The hospital will treat all patients the same, whether they share my faith, some other religion, or no religion.

Churches, on the other hand, often speak of loving people. It is in our marching orders, "Love your neighbor; love your enemy" (Matthew 5:43-44). I have often said that churches are hospitals for sinners. All of us, who profess faith in Christ and attend a church, have some sickness in our souls. Call it herniated hearts. And hopefully, when you come to a church, you will find smiling, caring people who leave their mark, not on your bandage, but on your heart.

Balloons Belong in Church

I have said it from the pulpit, and I am not taking it back. What I have said from the pulpit that I am not taking back is this: "Balloons belong in church." I have said it because balloons are for celebrations, and church should be a celebration. So, I stand by what I have said, but I would like to revise it slightly. Balloons belong in church, but not on Sunday morning in the sanctuary— and especially not hovering over the pulpit as the preacher preaches!

To our church members who missed that particular Sunday, I told you so. I told you to show up every Sunday because you never know what you might miss. It seems a child had released a balloon on Wednesday night in the sanctuary and with helium (and some hot air) it went to the ceiling. No problem. We have a high ceiling. Rethink that—big problem.

This particular balloon apparently had a good personality and got pleasure out of seeing the preacher sweat. The balloon was like an airplane in a holding pattern, circling the airport (pulpit). It almost landed then went back up for another go round. I can see every set of eyes in the sanctuary, and trust me, they were not on me. That may be a good thing, but it meant that they were not listening to me. So, what's new?

I think my parishioners actually enjoyed it—anything to break the boredom. Raise your hand if you have ever chuckled when a kid fell off a pew, or the organ wheezed, or the sound system picked up police calls. Do you watch The Weather Channel when it's 68 degrees and sunny around the country? No, but I'll bet you watch during hurricanes.

A minister went to the Talladega 500, and after watching the cars circle the track for hours, boredom set in and turned him into the worst sinner. He admitted that voices within him began to hope for a smashup, a fire, anything to break the monotony. How could he as a minister hope to see cars flip and smash into walls? The demon of boredom had gotten the best of him.

Maybe you are like the millions of Christians who have settled into the comfortable belief that boredom at church is one of the crosses we carry. If you are one of those, then a balloon hovering over the pulpit was more excitement than you ever imagined could happen between stained glass windows.

I am not saying that worship should be entertaining, but we should strive to do it well. We preachers should work on our craft as a good surgeon works on his. (I don't want a surgeon practicing on me like we practice on our parishioners.) We should work to make worship interesting and compelling so that worshippers don't need a hovering balloon to have Sunday lunch conversation about church.

"We had to miss church today. How was it?" "It was great," says the hungry parishioner. "Balloons again?" "No," he says, "just a great sermon."

Now I'm really dreaming.

The Most Interesting Minister in the World

We Baptists claim not to care for beer, but we do laugh at the beer commercials. One in particular, recently, has put a smile on our faces. "The Most Interesting Man in the World" commercials depict an older, handsome, bearded man with Spanish music playing softly in the background. The narrator describes this man ("the most interesting in the world"), who just happens to like a certain brand of brew, in this way:
• His mother wears a tattoo that says "son."
• He once taught a German shepherd to bark in Spanish.
• If he punched you in the face, you would have to fight the urge to thank him.
• Both sides of his pillow are cool.

Well, a friend of mine (Brett Younger) came up with a list for "the most interesting minister in the world."[2] That list includes:
• When the most interesting minister leads a silent prayer, the birds stop singing.

---

[2] Brett Younger, "Baptists Today" (October, 2010) 28.

- When the most interesting minister steps into the baptistery, the waters part.
- When the most interesting minister preaches, cell phones refuse to ring.
- When the most interesting minister performs a wedding ceremony, no one looks at the bride.

Well, I just got back from a week's vacation at the beach, and trust me, I am not the "most interesting minister in the world." I spent a week hanging out at a pool, napping, watching movies, napping, playing golf, napping, and winning the family Putt Putt contest (though by only a stroke over my wife). If you think that was interesting, then you would enjoy watching paint dry.

Most of us ministers lead normal lives. They look a lot like your life. Bills have to be paid, the oil needs changing, we fuss over what to buy for back-to-school, marital spats happen, etc. We get mad at the golf course (which I did on vacation) when the dad gum ball won't go where it is supposed to go.

However, we ministers should lead lives that aren't exactly normal. We (and others) should strive to lead exemplary lives. We can't just blow it off every time we make a mistake and say, "Oh, we are only human." We who preach should practice what we preach. And those in the pews who claim to follow Christ should do so as well. We ministers should say what the Apostle Paul says: "Join in imitating me, and observe those who live according to the example you have in us" (Philippians 3:17). Though we don't always say eloquent things in the pulpit (or on paper), we should be able to say to our congregation, "Watch me, follow how I live, and you will be OK." Not perfect, but OK.

But I would like to be "the most interesting minister," just for one Sunday. Why? Because his sermons are never long enough.

Stuttttttering Like Mmmmel Tttttillis

I sent Glenn a text that said, "The chimes at 3:00 sounded like Mel Tillis trying to talk." His response to me was, "Still ttttrying to figure out the problem." Glenn is our Minister of Music, and I sent him the text because the church's carillon, which plays chimes on the hour, is broken and sounds like Otis from the Andy Griffith Show. The dictionary definition of carillon is: "A sanctuary set of chromatically tuned bells in a tower, usually played from a keyboard." Ours is not played from a keyboard.

We actually have a little man who lives up in our steeple. We send him food from time to time and offer him free parking at church for his services. Apparently he has some issues with claustrophobia or perhaps the ringing in his ears has made him nuts. But for whatever reason, the bells aren't ringing as bells should ring, so the chiming of the hour sounds more like an old 45 record that is "stuck."

Actually, our carillon is played by a CD. We could do some fun things, by the way, with our CD-run carillon if we choose to. We could, I suppose, play Elvis' greatest hit on his birthday or "Sweet Home Alabama" and turn it up so loud our friends in Ranburne, Alabama could enjoy it.

Another possible use of the carillon would be to set a downtown mood each day, depending, of course, on the mood of the preacher, yours truly. If I am in a bad mood, then I will give the community a steady diet of Roseanne Barr singing the National Anthem. If I am sleepy, then you get Barry Manilow's greatest hits. Right now, with our carillon imitating a talking Mel Tillis, I'm thinking folks at the downtown square are a tad nervous all day.

Come to think of it, the carillon in the steeple mirrors in many ways those who gather beneath it. Stuttering, stammering people are welcome at church. Most of us struggle with putting words (stuttering is no laughing matter) and life together. All of us have our own set of faults, now don't we? The truth is, all of us who gather beneath the steeple for worship stutter to talk and stammer to live. We all walk with a limp. None of us who gather beneath the steeple have it all together. Yes, we are happy because we know Christ, and we want to know Him better and serve Him more faithfully. But, our lives often match our now stuttering chimes. They can play beautiful music at times (so can we), but at other times, they struggle (so do we) to get it all together.

People are attracted to our steeple because it rises above the Carrollton landscape or because they hear the (normally beautiful) chimes. Who comes to the steeple? People who are hurting, stuttering, stammering, lonely, sad, broken, and confused, that's who. They come to the steeple because they hope that beneath the steeple is a sanctuary where they can find rest and hope.[3]

This Sunday I hope you will take your stuttering, stammering self to the church of your choice. "But Moses said to the Lord...I am slow of speech and slow of tongue" (Exodus 4: 10). Maybe Moses is the little man in our steeple.

Prison or Parish?

It might seem like an easy decision: jail or church? I read with a chuckle a recent article about what is happening in Bay Minette, Alabama, where non-violent offenders will have that choice. It is called Operation Restore our Community. The city judge there will let misdemeanor offenders choose to go to a place of worship for a year or go to jail and pay a fine. If the offender completes the one-year church attendance requirement, then the case will be dismissed.

---

[3] Charles Poole, *Don't Cry Past Tuesday* (Macon: Smyth & Helwys, 1991) 8.

Maybe it is not such an easy decision. It might depend on who is preaching. I've heard some sermons that bordered on torture (including some of mine). I wonder if the judge might reduce the sentence depending on the quality of the preaching and singing. I've heard some really awful singing in church, the kind that makes you grab the pew and hold on. Can the offender appeal to the judge if the singing gets unbearable?

What if he picked a church where the preacher takes great pride in beating folks up with words? It's not true, you know: "Sticks and stones may break my bones, but words will never hurt me." It never has been true, and I have heard preachers work folk over like Mike Tyson did an opponent in the ring. And just when the hapless sinner is on the ropes, another zinger. So, can the offender go to the judge and ask for a change of venue if he is battered by an angry preacher?

I've been to some churches where you were not made to feel welcome unless you looked or dressed a certain way. What if he wears prison stripes to church, and the looks he gets say, "You're not welcome." Wouldn't we all have to be willing to let him sit by us in church? We don't have a section roped off that says, "For prisoners only." So, if he is not welcomed warmly, can he then go back to the judge and say, "I'll take prison."

You see, I'm just thinking of what a challenge that agreement would put on a church. The responsibility would fall squarely on our shoulders to be the kind of church that welcomes the prisoner, the outcast, and the troubled soul. We would need hearts of compassion to try and understand how he got to where he is in life—someone who has lived outside the law and made bad choices. In other words, we would have to practice what we preach.

I have a hunch that most churches I know around here would pass the test. I believe we would roll out the welcome mat. So yes, the would-be prisoner can have a seat on any pew next to the rest of us sinners.

But if that happens, please don't say, "Well, aren't you going to tithe?" In fact, tithing to a church that has bad preaching and singing may feel like paying a fine.

A Man and His Dog

He made me laugh, and I immediately felt a connection with him. Forget for the moment that he was dying from cancer and had at best a few weeks or a month to live. I liked his candor and good humor. A little dog, yapping at the top of her lungs, greeted me at the front porch of the man's trailer. I have forgotten the dog's name, but Hyper, would fit. He apologized for the dog's seeming hostility to strangers, and then with a wry smile said this: "I give her coffee in the morning, Mountain Dew in the afternoon, and a margarita at night." I almost fell out.

I have met some of the most wonderful and interesting people through Hospice. Several local ministers serve as Hospice chaplains, going to see patients who request a minister. I don't get called a lot. Sometimes I begrudge going, because I think I'm so busy that I don't have time. But the truth is, I never seem to regret the visits. My life is enriched by being around people who are facing death just around the corner. I am inspired by their honesty and courage.

One time I visited a man who had been in Vietnam and he had a confession to make. He made it to me. He had killed some innocent people in the war and needed to tell someone before he died, and I just happened to be that someone. I was overwhelmed by his words.

I almost feel unworthy to talk to folk who are dying. Many of them have had tough lives and more hardships than I can imagine, and they just want to talk to someone before they die.

Others are too young to be dying. Those are the toughest.

Some have questions about God and why this is happening to them. You know, "Why me? Why this? Why now?" They have questions for which I have no answers.

Others will say "I'm alright with the man upstairs." I have never been fond of calling God "the man upstairs," but when a person is on their deathbed, it seems perfectly alright.

Back to the wonderful man with the dog, a dog high on caffeine and margaritas. My visit with him was brief, but I was touched by his thankful heart. A few friends had done some kind things for him, such as putting gravel in his driveway. He was humbled that friends would do stuff for him in his dying days. I left his trailer feeling like I had made a new friend. I said, "I've got to come back and see him again."

But the weekend came, and the busy guy got busy. I got a call from Hospice late on Monday saying he was getting worse, and he had asked if I could come back. I couldn't go Tuesday, after all, I am quite busy. I told them I would go out on Wednesday afternoon. He died Wednesday morning. Dang it.

I never got to make that follow-up visit. He must have felt he needed to talk to me before he died, and I sure felt like I needed to talk to him again. But a thing called death (and my busy schedule) got in the way.

Fall Back

It was our second stop, and the kind lady said, "It will be ten or fifteen minutes." We had already been to one restaurant after church, and the nice lady there said, "It will be about forty minutes." That's why we left that one and went to the second eating establishment, where she said, "ten or fifteen minutes." I don't know if she was deliberately lying, trying to keep us from leaving, but the "ten or fifteen minutes" turned into one hour before we were seated. One whole hour! And by the way, it just happened to be the Sunday of the time change—you know, the day your clocks "fall back" or as we say, you gain an hour. So, what did you do with the hour you gained? I spent mine waiting on a table for lunch.

I remember reading several years ago, that scientists had added a "leap second" to the world's clocks. Actually, what happened was, our clocks slowed down one second and the world gained a second. Did you notice? I missed that one. According to scientists, the earth's rotation varies slightly, and as a result, our means of measuring time (watches, grandfather clocks, etc.), have to be altered accordingly. So, if the earth's rotation really does vary from "time to time," then that might explain why I sometimes feel that the world is spinning really fast around me. It might also explain why there are times (really boring, long sermons, for example) when time seems to stand still.

I am reminded of what Al (Einstein, that is) said. He had a theory that we call the "clock paradox," which (I think) is that time passes more slowly for an object in motion than for one at rest. (To any scientist reading this, forgive me. Call me or e-mail me with your corrections.) To put it in church terms, we would stay a lot younger by giving ourselves fully to meaningful ecclesiastical activities—that is, to prayer, caring about others, and giving to charity (or to church, can you say stewardship?), than by sitting on our duffs.

All I know is this: I have lots of wonderful church folk who are, shall we say, not spring chickens anymore. But, by golly, so many of them just seem to keep right on going, well into their nineties. They live right, they care about others, and they give of their time and resources, i.e., they stay busy doing healthy, wholesome activities. They do it out of deeply held Christian convictions. I'm not nearly as smart as Einstein, but I could have reached his "clock paradox" by observing church folk in the lab of real life.

The Apostle Paul put it this way in Ephesians 5:15-16 (Phillips): "Live life, then, with a due sense of responsibility, not as men (and women) who do not know the meaning and purpose of life but as those who do. Make the best use of your time, despite all the difficulties of these days."

As we sat and sat and sat waiting on a table at a restaurant, I thought to myself, "Einstein was right. I'm aging quickly (while at rest) as the hour I gained last night is being taken back." Okay, let me 'fess up. What I really thought can't be printed in a Christian book.

Safety First

I pass along this information to you well in advance of the start of the college football season. I do so out of concern for your safety and well being. You have now been warned and have time to adequately prepare. What I am warning you about is a new study that shows that when your team wins a close game, you have a higher risk of dying on the way home. The study showed that traffic deaths rise dramatically in the home town of winning teams on game day. The author states that "going from a blow-out (game) to a nail-biter increases observed fatalities by 133 %...It may be fair to say that, on any given day, the danger of a close game is as detrimental as the absence of seat belt laws." So, if you want to stay safe, avoid close college football games this fall.

We as a society have gone nuts over safety. We have home security systems and floodlights, plus a ferocious dog to guard our place. Seat belts aren't enough for our cars; we now have airbags and automatic locks. We "baby proof" our homes to keep our precious children safe. Well, you get the point.

I have more information on safety that might interest you. To really be safe, you should avoid riding in automobiles because they account for 20% of all fatal accidents. On the other hand, to ensure safety, you can't stay at home, because 17% of all accidents occur at home. If you choose to walk on the sidewalk or streets, be aware that 14% of all accidents happen to pedestrians. So, that is not a safe choice either. Neither is traveling by air, rail, or water because 16% of all accidents involve these forms of transportation. That leaves 33%. Guess what? Thirty-two percent of all deaths occur in hospitals. At all costs, avoid hospitals.

There is some good news in all this paranoia. Are you ready for this? Only .001% of all deaths occur in worship services in church, and these are usually related to some previous physical disorder. It is a fact that a lot of church folk thought that bad preaching would "do them in," but so far no direct link between a bad homily and the death of the saints has been ascertained. So, logic would tell us that worship is a very safe place to be.

Church should also be a safe place emotionally and spiritually. I quote an old Ken Medema song: "If this (church) is not a place where my heart cries can be heard, where can I go to speak?" The song continues its honest confession in a later line: "I don't need another place for always wearing smiles, even when it's not the way I feel." The church should be a place where your tears are understood and where you can share your heart's biggest ache. I want people to feel safe at church—safe to confess, safe to be honest, and safe to be loved.

See you Sunday in the church of your choice. It could save your life!

Butter Fingers

Lots of people said, "At least it wasn't the juice." People after church said it. Friends at lunch said the same thing. The reason people said, "At least it wasn't the juice," is because during communion on Sunday, I dropped the bread. Not just a piece of bread. Not just a crumb. No, I dropped enough bread to make the Flowers Bakery people cringe. I dropped an entire plate of it on the floor of the sanctuary, which of course, made me want to find sanctuary somewhere, anywhere else on the planet. It didn't make a lot of noise, thank goodness, only the sound of the plate hitting the carpet. But there were about, oh, 92 or 106, (who's counting?) little pieces of bread scattered on the floor in front of the communion table.

It reminded me of what I have told a bride and groom at a wedding rehearsal: "If we drop the ring or rings, don't bend over and pick them up. Just go on as if nothing has happened. Nobody will notice or hear them drop; just pretend it didn't happen." Well, when you drop a plate of bread in front of God and everybody, you can't pretend it didn't happen. There were a few gasps, as if someone had seen the Holy Ghost. There were a few smiles, as if to say, "I want to laugh out loud (LOL) but I'm in church and this is, after all, holy communion, so am I going to Hades if I just smile?" I don't think I gasped, but I did mutter something under my breath. I have been assured that I didn't say a dirty word. Our service is on the radio, and I'm glad that I didn't utter something akin to what I have uttered over an errant golf shot.

I'm trying to forget my, oh so public *faux pas*, but my kind, loving church members won't let me. We went to lunch after church and were talking to some of those who aren't going to let me forget. We were standing by their table, and it just so happened that the waitress brought them their bread. Great timing! They said, "Want some bread? Oh, don't drop it."

I'm sure I won't hear the end of it this side of Heaven. One of our deacons, years ago, dropped an offering plate. I haven't let him forget it; so turn about is fair play. By the way, when he dropped the plate, people were grabbing the money on the way down. They sort of felt like, I guess, that this was the Lord's way of giving it back to them.

We all make mistakes, but when you make one in front of a few hundred people, now that is a doozie. Our mistakes tend to haunt us, especially when others remind us of them. Forgiving ourselves is one of life's greatest challenges and toughest things to do. It is easier when those closest to us offer us their forgiveness and when we base our lives on God's grace and not our own goodness. When we accept our own imperfections, we become candidates for grace. Then we find it easier to offer grace to others, even to yours truly, who in his younger days, had better hands.

"And be ye kind to one another, tenderhearted, forgiving one another, as God in Christ has forgiven you" (Ephesians 4:32).

Owing the Methodists

There are some funny answers and some serious answers to the question. The question is: What are necessary evils? Funny answers go like this: lobbyists, Wal-Mart, fast-food, curfew, mothers-in-law, and lawyers. The more serious answers are: war and taxes.

Being a church guy, I know of one that you have not thought of: church buses. You have to have them, but they are always breaking down. Have you ever been on a church trip, using a church bus, when it didn't end up on the side of the road? We took our big church bus on a children's trip one summer. It broke down. And of course, we paid big bucks to have the big bus repaired. We took the same bus on a children's trip to South Carolina. And how did the children wind up in the Wal-Mart parking lot? You guessed it. The bus broke down.

Well, as it turned out, our youth were leaving the next day for a trip and needed the bus. We were desperate to find transportation. And in a big hurry. What do you do when facing a crisis? Call the Methodists, as in First Methodist, just a stone's throw from our parking lot. And boy did they come to our rescue. They have a bus that they loaned us, and for that we are grateful. To show our gratitude all of us Baptists have agreed to be sprinkled.

Their bus worked great, once we got the snakes out of it. (I thought only Baptists were snake handlers.) And we had to remove the life size cut-out of John Wesley from the front passenger seat. Well, there was one problem: the driver said that every time it passed a Hooters restaurant, the bus veered in that direction. I'm just reporting what he said.

Seriously, we share lots of good stuff with our Methodist neighbors besides buses and pigeons. We share a common faith. Our beliefs are actually very similar. We share a common commitment to witness for Christ in this community and a common commitment to help the needy. We participate together in community services like Holy Week and Thanksgiving. We are friends who share a concern for one another and a sincere wish for the success of the other. I think the words of Paul to the church at Philippi are good words to all Christians in this community: "Do nothing from selfish ambition or conceit, but in humility regard others as better than yourselves. Let each of you look not to your own interests, but to the interests of others" (2:3-4).

And so, with that in mind, if the Methodists ever need our bus, they can have it. However, ours doesn't veer towards Hooters, it veers towards liquor stores. We just hope nobody sees us in there. Of course, I'm kidding. Baptists don't go to liquor stores, at least not in buses.

"How Was Church?"

I simply asked, "How was church?" I asked because I stayed home recovering from knee surgery, while Sheri and Natalie went. It almost never happens that I am at home during church listening to the service on the radio. When I'm not preaching, we are on vacation. So, it was highly unusual for me to be home, while my family was at church. And thus the question, "How was it?"

I certainly didn't expect the answer I got. I expected, "Fine." I expected, "Sunday school was great. We learned about..." I expected, "So and so asked about you." What I didn't expect was, "Somebody stepped on my donut at Sunday school." I got that response from Natalie, not Sheri, by the way. I guess Sheri, too, would have been upset about her donut, but that would not have made her list of "what happened at church?"

For an eight-year-old, what's important is not the Sunday school lesson, who was there, who was not there, etc. What's important is what happened to her donut. What is important to an eight-year-old is not the same as what is important to adults. Call it the gap.

For some, it is wide as the Grand Canyon. For others (saints), it is as small as a thimble. I'm talking about the gap between what matters to God and what matters to us. What matters to God is spelled out in Micah 6:8—things like "walking humbly with God, loving kindness, and doing justice." But what matters to us?

My list of what matters changes from year to year, depending on circumstances. For example, since we have an eight-year-old, what matters to me is what she is learning, and teaching her how to live a good, Christian life. Other things that matter to me are handwritten notes, anniversaries, college football, golf, and this is really important, getting a clean bill of health at my annual medical check-up. My relationships with my wife, kids, and church members matter to me. In today's financial times, our retirement accounts matter, as does the price of gasoline and Wall Street bailouts. Sometimes, however, there are things that matter to me that get way too much attention and some things that should matter more, that don't get enough attention.

It seems to me that a good way to measure our spiritual growth would be to measure the size of the gap—that is, the gap between what matters to God and what matters to us. What matters to God is that we walk humbly with Him, that we love kindness, and practice justice. And if those aren't anywhere on our list of what matters, then something is way out of balance in our lives.

And if somebody stepping on our donut really matters, then the gap is way too big.

"That Guy"

Every Sunday I do a "sermon in a sack," which is a cute name for the children's sermon. Lots of precious little kids skip down the church's aisle and plop down in front of me, eagerly waiting to discover the contents in "the sack." Okay, eagerly might be a tad strong. Each Sunday I try not to disappoint. There is an object in the sack—baseball, alarm clock, hammer—some object that becomes a sermon for the kids.

One recent Wednesday night I asked one of those kids, Cam, if his mom was at church. He said "no," and that was that. But Cam went home that night and told his mom, "That guy who does the thing in the sack was looking for you." So, I am now "That guy who does the thing in the sack." I am known, at least to Cam, for something I do.

I am not "Pastor Steve" or Ms. Sheri's husband, or Tyler and Natalie's dad. No, to Cam, I am "that guy." It could be a lot worse. I remember preachers who were my pastors, and I know it could be so much worse. I could be "that guy who wears the same suit every Sunday." Or how would I like it if Cam had said, "that guy who has a Bible as big as Turner Field." I guess I should take some solace in being the sack guy.

We are known for what we do. And for what we say. Cam doesn't really know me well enough to know how charming, witty, kind, and intelligent I am. Those who know me well would dispute the charming part…and the rest. So, he knows me by what he has seen me do.

I don't want to sound cheesie, but the statement that comes to mind is one I learned in Sunday school as a kid: "You are the only Bible some people will ever read." If we are known to Cam and scores of kids like him by what we do and say, then be careful what you do and say. Don't do or say anything that would do harm or present a bad impression to a kid.

It's not a bad thing, by the way, to be known for what you do. "She's the lady who works at the Soup Kitchen." "He's the kind man who gives me a smile at church." "That's the teenager who took my groceries out to the car."

The children are watching us for sure. That's fine with me. Go ahead and watch me. Now, don't get me wrong, I'm not perfect; I know that and my wife and kids know it for sure. I have a few church members fooled, but for the most part, they know me. I try to be transparent.

For a lot of people, religious people especially, and Christians for sure, there is a gap as wide as the Chattahoochee River between the artificial and the authentic. The more authentic we are, then the closer we are to God. The more artificial we are, the closer we are to the Pharisees. Let's all strive to be authentically, not artificially, Christian.

As for the kids, I think it was Robert Fulghum who said it best: "Don't worry that they won't listen, worry that they are always watching." Well, I know they are watching "the sack guy."

"A Week without SpongeBob"

Our then six-year-old described our recent mission trip, with a look of horror in her eyes, as "A week without SpongeBob." It was more than she could bear. I described it as a week without Sportscenter. So, what's the difference?

We took a group of church folk, myself, wife, and daughter included, on a mission trip to a coal-mining town in Kentucky. Well, they used to mine coal, but don't anymore, and so the little town is as dead as Mayberry. We didn't have access to a TV, and so our daughter groaned about her plight—life for a week without her favorite TV show, "SpongeBob SquarePants." And for me, a week without Sportscenter, and even more importantly, I missed all the coverage of the U.S. Open golf tournament. Oh, the sacrifices we make.

I tried to teach our daughter about what we do on mission trips and why we go. We go "to help people," and "tell them about God." So, I said, "This week is not about you." Therefore, don't complain about where we are staying or what we are eating. This is not a Holiday Inn Express kind of experience and there are no McDonalds with chicken fingers. In other words, I talked to her about sacrifice, all the while grumbling under my breath that we should be able to schedule a mission trip at a time that doesn't conflict with some of the greatest sporting events. After all, I'm the pastor and surely I can have more input into the church schedule so that we can "help people" at times that are more convenient for me and my Tiger Woods fetish.

While trying to teach our daughter the lessons of sacrifice, I learned a lesson from Cathy. Cathy is a fifty-something widow who lives in that small Kentucky town. I, and some others, did home repair for her. Admittedly, I'm not much at home repair. I figure God made plumbers and sheetrockers for a reason. However, I learned to do sheetrock (which is a really hard job), mudding, and sanding on this trip. Thank goodness I had a good teacher. It was kind of fun to learn a new trade, and if the preaching gig doesn't work out, then coming to a store front near you: Davis Drywall and Home Repair.

Anyway, when Cathy heard I was a preacher, she wanted my full attention. She got it. She wanted me to pray for her (somehow she has the mistaken notion that my prayers are more effective than yours), and she was eager to tell me her story.

I listened intently to her gut-wrenching story, and the thought that went through my head was "Steve, you don't know jack about sacrifice. Get out your pencil and take notes. She's about to teach you something." Her husband had died four years ago from cancer. But before that, some 21 years before that, is when the accident happened. The accident at the coal mine left him with brain damage and permanent blindness. And so for 21 years, she cared for her invalid husband. Twenty one years. Not one week or one month, but 21 dad gum years. And then, by the way, if that wasn't enough to deal with, he got sick with cancer and died. And so that is her story. That's Cathy's story. And I was glad to do some sheetrock work for her and glad that my path happened to cross hers.

I thought that a week without Sportscenter was a sacrifice. Boy, did I have a lot to learn. It was a good mission trip for at least two reasons: One, I learned to sheetrock and two, I learned about sacrifice. And I learned them both at Cathy's house.

Addicted to...

Conner is six-years-old, and he has an addiction. He spilled his soul to me recently in my office. Six-years-old and he's hooked. Drugs? Alcohol? What is it? Corn. He's addicted to corn. The boy loves corn, and in his words, "I'm addicted." I love corn, and so I challenged him to a corn-eating contest. He said he could whip me, and I happen to believe him.

I have a theory about vegetables, by the way. I love vegetables that have one syllable—corn, peas, beans. If they have more than one syllable, and heaven forbid, more than one word, then watch out. Brussels sprouts, for example don't have a chance to make it to my plate, because it is two words and three syllables. Anyway, I love corn as much as Conner, but I wouldn't use the word addicted to describe my passion for it.

The word addict may best describe my feelings, however, about football. I do love it. I should check into the Betty Ford Clinic for Football Addicts to get some help. I'm not the best husband in the world during football season (as opposed to other times in the year). I am like an addict on weekends. I can't seem to put down the remote; it's like trying to pass on the dessert table at a church dinner on the grounds.

When our son was little, a deacon in a former church taught him how to make a small football out of paper, and then how to flick it with your fingers. It worked great—too great. We were eating out one night, and he flicked the paper football at me. I was holding up two fingers as if they were goal posts. He was to flick the ball through the goal post, but instead flicked it into the hair (it looked like a gray beehive) of the older lady at the table next to us. That's the kind of thing that happens when you are addicted to football.

Actually, real addiction is not a laughing matter. I don't pretend to understand it, but I feel real sympathy for those who battle addictions. The big three addictions, some say, are money, sex, and power. No wonder the monastics vowed poverty, chastity, and obedience. I wonder how would it feel to be controlled by something that is destroying your life, and yet, you feel powerless to stop? I admire people who work with addicts, whether through AA, some other organization, or personal counseling.

Some might say that our addiction to sports is as destructive to the family as these others. Lots of men (and women) neglect their families because the remote control controls them, especially during football season. Others gamble away the family income on sporting events.

I struggle, like a lot of you do, with being a good father, husband, and pastor when other things, like football, take too much of my time and attention. Well, if addiction is a bad word, then moderation is a good word. The Bible calls it "self-control" (Galatians 5:23). And yes, moderation in eating corn is good too, but it won't help you beat the pastor in a corn-eating contest.

"And the winner Is..."

"Steve Davis." I've been winning stuff like crazy lately. I used to say what you say, and that is, "I've never won anything in my life."

I used to say it because it was true. Our Rotary club has a weekly raffle, where members buy a ticket, and the winning ticket is picked out of a hat. The winner gets a gift certificate or cash, but the proceeds go towards some local charity or service project. I had entered for years and never won. That's why I said, "I've never won anything in my life."

But now I am winning everything. About six weeks ago I won the raffle at Rotary and got a rocking chair. Perhaps that was rigged, as a subtle hint, given my age and having a six-year-old. But I think not. A week later I won a door prize, a cooler, at a golf tournament. Then, a few weeks ago, I won the "big daddy" of them all. Our Rotary club had a membership contest and at the end of it, some lucky someone would have their name drawn and would get a flat-screen TV. Guess who that lucky someone was? Yep, the guy who never wins anything took home the big prize. I didn't have a flat-screen, by the way, while all my friends watched football games and The Masters on theirs. Jealous? A bit. To top off my winning spree, the dessert if you will, this week at the Tanner Medical Center Volunteers' Banquet, I won an Elvis CD.

All of which leads me to the Bible. If you are going to camp out anywhere in the Bible, I would not suggest Deuteronomy. Actually, I would suggest the gospels as a good place to hang out. But back to the fifth book in the Bible and the theology in it. There is a belief system espoused there, called Deuteronomic Theology, which teaches that the righteous win everything, including raffles at Rotary and Elvis CDs. It teaches (Ch. 28) that the righteous have nice houses, beautiful spouses, great kids, good health, and flat-screens (and the obvious inference, since I am winning everything, is that I am in that category). Meanwhile, the unrighteous, have to suffer with living in shacks, ugly wives, bad kids, bad health, and black/white TVs. And that's the way life works. Simple huh?

Such thinking can be found elsewhere in scripture, but it is found most prominently in Deuteronomy. In the New Testament, Jesus approached a man who was blind. Jesus' disciples asked the question about nice houses, beautiful spouses, and flat-screens. They phrased it like this: "Who sinned this man or his parents that he was born blind" (John 9: 2)? Jesus said, "Neither..."

There are preachers in this land who preach Deuteronomic Theology, but they call it something else. They call it the prosperity gospel. It's the same thing; they just call it something else. In that gospel, the faithful get rich, have nice houses, and flat-screens. The unrighteous? Too bad. Suffer with your old, thick, not-so-clear TV picture. Preachers who preach the prosperity gospel are "flat-out" wrong. They should read the whole Bible.

I have a list. It is a list of faithful believers who have suffered greatly. It's a long list. In fact, if I started in this column, it would stretch from here to the classified section. On the other hand, I have another long list on which are the names of the righteous who don't have much stuff—never have and never will. My recent winning streak has nothing to do with being righteous (ask my wife), though I would like to believe otherwise.

Over the years, when I have mentioned that I would like for us to purchase a flat-screen TV, Sheri has said something like this: How could we justify that when so many in our world have so little? I think she is the real Christian in our house. And I think she has read the whole Bible.

Origins of Popular Sayings

I say phrases all the time that I have no idea from whence they came. I say things like "I was scared as all get-out." "All-get-out" seems to be a Southern phrase used to indicate a high degree of something, as in "He was mad as all get-out."

Apparently, the first appearance of "all get-out" was in Mark Twain's "Huckleberry Finn," but its origin seems to be unknown. It must be connected somehow with "get out" or "leave." As a minister, after last week's Holy Week, I was "tired as all get-out."

I also don't know the origin of the phrase, "Two's company, three's a crowd." Though I do not know the exact origin of it, I do know who first said it. It was first said by a dad who attempted to go shopping for clothes with his wife and 10-year-old daughter. I also know it was first uttered about 15 minutes into that shopping spree/disaster.

What was I thinking? What I was thinking was that it would be cool to show my support for my daughter by participating in the buying of clothes for her. When our son was growing up, clothes were not a really big deal. He wore jeans or khakis, t-shirts, golf shirts, etc., but I had no desire to help him pick out his clothes. He didn't need or want my help. If I bought him clothes for Christmas he would promptly return them for the post-Christmas sale.

I don't know what would possess me then to think that with our daughter it would be any different. Having a little girl, (oops, young lady), is different. I actually enjoy picking out cute clothes for her to wear. I think I have a pretty good idea of what would look good on her. So, I mistakenly thought that my ideas and my presence would be welcomed on a shopping spree.

I have been wrong about a lot of things in my life, but I have never been so wrong about anything. About fifteen minutes into this experiment, I realized the shopping spree test tube had the wrong mix. The phrase: "Two's company, three's a crowd," came to mind. I was the "three."

I innocently made a couple of suggestions of clothes that I thought were cute, and Natalie and Sheri looked at me like I was Dennis Rodman's fashion designer. I promptly walked away and made no other suggestions. I will make other mistakes in my life as a parent, but I will not make that one again.

Showing love to our kids is easy. We go to their ballgames, music concerts, art exhibits, and church events and we cheer for them, we applaud them, we hug and affirm them. At times, however, the best way to show our love for them is by recognizing when it is time to stay out of their business. I don't like being the "three" on a shopping spree, but I was.

King Solomon had 700 wives and I am guessing lots of kids. He had all the money in the world and certainly took some of his 10-year-olds to the Jerusalem Shopping Center. And thus he coined these timely words: "Get wisdom, and whatever else you get, get insight" (Proverbs 4:7). I got "insight" the hard way.

By the way, I wanted to say to Natalie, "Don't look a gift horse in the mouth," since I am that "gift horse." But that is another phrase for another day.

Anniversary Anxiety

I have a line I use that gets a few laughs. As our wedding anniversary approached, people asked, "How many?" I responded with, "We've had eighteen wonderful years together. Of course, we have been married twenty." Truth is, we've had twenty good years together, mostly because she is "gooder" than I.

Our twentieth was celebrated with a couple of nights at Chateau Elan, a beautiful resort with golf, hiking trails and spa. We did all three (I highly recommend the spa massage) and had a really good, romantic get-away. Admittedly, I am not much of a romantic. Listening to a Barry Manilow tune while sitting in the Target parking lot before an anniversary shopping spree, is about as good as it gets. By the way, our last eight or so anniversaries have been spent at baseball parks, eating concession stand hot dogs, watching our son play.

Our tenth anniversary, as I recall, was not one for the record books. Though we did take a cruise later that summer to celebrate, the actual date of our anniversary (June 18) didn't turn out so well. After a meal at Outback, we drove to Atlanta to buy some new furniture. (How romantic.) Her idea, not mine. Though not greatly enthused about furniture shopping, I submitted graciously to her request. "Let's go to Macy's," she said, "there is one at Town and Country Mall." Why we had to go to this particular Macy's, I didn't know, but being our anniversary, I didn't ask. I had some bad vibes about this little excursion, but I love her enough to let her learn from her mistakes.

So, with Barry Manilow cranking out tunes, we headed for Macy's. We drove and drove and drove. Being our anniversary, I didn't complain. I hadn't learned a lot in ten years, but I had learned that. When we road-weary romantics arrived at Macy's, we asked the first clerk we saw, "Where is your furniture department?" Answer: "We don't sell furniture at *this* Macy's." Silence. Steve chuckles. Sheri is speechless (hard to believe).

Our anniversary excursion was beginning to look a lot like life. Real life. Life that doesn't turn out the way you planned. What to do? We headed to the men's section where I got new shorts and shirts for Father's Day and then to the ladies section where Sheri got a new swimsuit. After that, the long trek home, without furniture, but with Barry Manilow alongside. And with Barry's help, we turned a bad evening into a good one.

Maybe it is a bit cheesy to say that "when life deals you lemons, you make lemonade." Real life is hard sometimes, and finding the good in it and turning defeats into victories is not as easy as the cliché seems to make it. Paul said that "all things work together for good..." (Romans 8:28). He didn't say all things are good, but he did say that "all things work together for good." I believe he is right about that, but then again, I don't know if he ever went furniture shopping on a wedding anniversary.

A-Roid

OK, I'm mad. I'm mad at some professional baseball players. Not all, but some. I don't know any of them personally, and I know we shouldn't judge them unfairly. But, I'm hacked off at some of them—some of them like A-Rod (Alex Rodriguez), Barry Bonds, Mark McGuire, and the list goes on and on. I'm mad because the steroids era in professional baseball has ruined the records. Apparently, lots of players took steroids in recent years, and they went from looking like The Incredible Yulk to The Incredible Hulk. Barney Fife became Arnold Schwarzenegger. And the baseballs started leaving the ballparks like Baptists leaving a casino—quickly. And now what do we do with the records? Baseball, and its hallowed Hall of Fame, is all about the numbers. Should Hammerin' Hank still have the home run record? So, that's why I'm mad.

The temptation to cheat is great in other professions as well. When we read about the corruption in the corporate world, we know that the temptation involves lots of money. When a governor is caught trying to sell the senator's seat, we understand the power of the almighty dollar.

Cheating, however, doesn't always involve money. We ministers can take sermon shortcuts using the internet to steal some one else's sermons, without giving them credit. Students cheat by taking information off the test of another student. I suppose that lots of cheaters in our world don't get caught. Some men cheat on their wives, and no one knows. Big wigs in corporate America cheat their clients or cheat on their taxes, and somehow, they get away with it.

It is alleged that in professional baseball, the powers that be—owners and high ranking baseball officials—knew that steroids was a big issue, but they looked the other way. They looked the other way because fans love the long ball. And when the fans are coming out to see Joe Blow hit it a country mile, that lines the pockets of everyone associated with the game. So, it is alleged, they looked the other way. And if they did, they have really hurt the game. And how can these players, in good conscience, go into Cooperstown, knowing that their numbers are tainted?

Looking back on my short and pathetic baseball career, it makes me wonder what I could have done with some steroids. I was so skinny; I could have used some muscle. My Little League team wore pin stripes, and I was so skinny I had only one pin stripe on my uniform. The baseball bat swung me. I'm just wondering if my career might have landed me in the Hall if I could have been as "juiced" as some of these modern players.

We all get tempted every day to lie, cheat, or steal. Maybe temptation, in the form of a needle, would have gotten the best of me if someone had offered me a shortcut to a better career. I know it's easy to judge others for their moments of weakness, when, in truth, we all have them. So, I'm trying not to judge A-Rod (A-Roid, as some call him), but I'm still mad because I love baseball, and the steroids era has taken something away from the game that can never be gotten back. An asterisk (* Steroids Era) by someone's name won't erase the damage.

"Buy truth, and do not sell it," says the writer of Proverbs (23:23). I wish it were for sale at the ole' ball park.

Back to School

It was a Wednesday night. Enough said. Wednesdays are long days for Baptist ministers; this particular one began at 8:00 in the morning and ended at close to 8:00 in the evening after Wednesday night church and meetings. I wanted to go home and take my shoes off. That's it. Just that alone would have pleased me greatly.

I couldn't, however, because my wife was running errands for school, and it was now my assignment to take the kids and do some "back to school" shopping for shoes (at 8:00 PM on a Wednesday!). And, oh by the way, did I tell you just how miserable I am at that time on Wednesday? I promise, if I could have just taken my shoes off I would have been the happiest minister this side of the 500 Club.

So, I took our then 17-year-old and five-year-old shoe shopping. I wanted to take mine (shoes) off, and they wanted some new ones. He, the 17-year-old, has to have new shoes at the start of a new school year (it must be a school rule), because he is dead set on it. The "tennis shoes" that he was wearing looked fine to me, but not to him. They were old and were hurting his feet, he said. I'll bet.

Buying shoes for kids is never as simple as it seems. I thought this time might actually go easy since he quickly picked up a pair that he liked, and they were priced reasonably, meaning somewhere less than an "arm and a leg." Guess what? They just happened to be out of his size. So, here we go, starting over.

Meanwhile, our five-year-old was taking everything off the rack in the store and giving commentary on it. I was "shoooshing" her to the point that I was completely out of patience, an item that I had in short supply at the beginning of this "back to school" shopping spree.

After considerable soul searching, our oldest found a second pair that he liked. Guess what? They just happened to cost $120! There seems to be something immoral about paying that much for sneakers. I'm not paying that even if I had just won the lottery, much less if it's a Wednesday night, and I felt like I had just been run over by a freight train.

I have told him time and time again, by the way, about my old Converse high-tops and how "cool" they were and how little they cost. I might as well be talking to a tree stump. He said he had a $10 off coupon (whoopee) but then couldn't find it. "I just had it," he said. We found it after we got back in the car. (Do these kinds of things only happen to us?)

We finally settled on a pair that was about half the price of the others. He held them up and asked me if I liked the way they looked. Huh? At that price, and at that point in my day, I would have liked anything. I was out of patience and ready to get home and take my old, well-worn shoes off. Our kids will learn that there are good times and there are bad times to get Dad to take them shopping. Wednesday night after church falls in the bad times category.

I know the Apostle Paul said that "love is patient" (1 Corinthians 13). I also know, however, that he never took kids shopping for shoes late on a Wednesday evening.

Baptismal Blues

I've performed a few hundred baptisms, I suppose. To those who aren't Baptist, we dunk, not sprinkle. We put them all the way under. For notorious sinners (names withheld to protect the guilty), we hold them under longer. There are days when I think we should sprinkle like our Methodist friends. A couple of Sundays ago was one of those days.

Getting ready for baptisms, which includes running the water in the baptistery (fancy name for pool), and putting on robes and waders, is no easy assignment. Yes, the minister wears waders, like hunters on a duck hunt. That way we stay dry, at least theoretically, so that we can get back quickly to the worship service. People who don't know that we wear waders think that we Baptist ministers are like Superman, changing in a phone booth and getting back to worship faster than a "speeding bullet."

We wear a white robe over the waders, one that is especially made for baptism, with a zipper up the front. I have two that I have worn for years. They are always in the closet that houses the robes. Always. Well, not that Sunday. As the young man who was being baptized put on his robe, I searched for mine in vain. A sense of panic set in. I had several hundred people waiting for the baptism and no robe.

Surely they had just been misplaced. Oh, there were two or three other robes in the closet, but they were for children and the Barney Fifes in our church. Because time was of the essence, I had no choice but to go with what I had. I've never done a baptism when the robe fit so tightly that I was turning blue and could barely breathe. Putting the robe on required a couple of cans of WD40, motor oil, and a girdle. Taking it off was worse. I needed some scissors and a chainsaw.

Where is reality TV when you need them? If they could secretly film us doing church, it would be a big hit. If only someone had been running a camera and had caught the baptismal fiasco on tape, I would have my own show.

We Baptists think that baptism is a beautiful outward symbol of what takes place in a person's heart when Christ comes in. And so we take it seriously. Back in 1527 in Switzerland, a man named Felix Manz was sentenced to be drowned because he refused to stop baptizing adults who professed faith in Christ. His accusers took him out in a boat, bound him hand and foot and dropped him over the side of the boat.

I believe in the symbol of baptism, but I don't think I'm willing to sink like an anchor for it. My drama over the disappearing baptismal robe is nothing compared to what Mr. Manz faced on that lake.

Now our church has the question of the missing robes. Does someone have a fetish for robes? Is there an underground market for them? Will they be listed on eBay? If you see them around town, let me know. Otherwise, I will at my next baptism, turn blue again, and once is enough.

Baptist Invasion

I write to invoke envy in my readers. Why envy? Well, I am using our son's laptop from the 26th floor of the Hilton Hawaiian Village, as I compose words for you. And the words I compose are inspired and thankful. Oh, they are not inspired as scripture is inspired, but they do come from a heart that has been touched. I am attending the Baptist World Alliance in Honolulu, a gathering of some 4,000 Baptist souls from 105 countries. Our church sent our family here for our 15th church anniversary, and thus the thankful and inspired words.

Honolulu hasn't quite known what to do with all these immersion-happy Christians. But these Baptists are not like the Bible belt ones that you and I know. To prove the point, I have been here a week, and I haven't had the first piece of fried chicken. At the first meeting, sitting directly behind us were six or seven young, college girls, who were as blonde as Britney Spears. I figured they either had to be from California or Norway. As soon as Norwegian words of praise to God came from their lips, I knew. So, yes, it is a different kind of meeting.

One of the greatest moments came opening night when we bowed our 4,000 heads simultaneously for prayer, and each prayed the Lord's Prayer in their native tongue. I prayed in southern, and drawing out my syllables, my Lord's Prayer finished a few moments later than the rest of the world's. But, I didn't miss the awesome spiritual experience. I suppose heaven will sound something like that.

The theme of this year's BWA is "Hear the Spirit." We Baptists have neglected to talk much of the Spirit for fear that we might start swinging from the church's chandeliers. The truth is, God's Spirit lives in all who profess faith in Christ, and that same Spirit should produce in all of us the normal Christian life. So, yours truly has spent a week listening to the Spirit, and I haven't jumped one pew in the process. But I have been given a heart that is overflowing with gratitude—for our church that sent us here (not a one-way ticket) and for God's goodness to me.

Hawaiians have some really cool words. Aloha, of course, means "hello" and "goodbye." Another cool one is mahalo, "thank you." Right now, sitting in a beautiful hotel room with my family, my heart is filled with a million mahalos. All I need to do now is take that cool Hawaiian word back home and live it. That's what I think the Spirit is saying to me at this moment.

And I apologize for the envy.

Baptists and Methodists

We all remember Mother's Day, 2008, because that is when the tornados hit Carrollton. We ministers remember it because the power went out all over town (including many churches) and many church members had trees on their homes. Lots of local churches cancelled services, I am told, because of the lack of electricity. Well, we decided to go ahead with church, without power, AC or a sound system. I remarked, with some humor, that First Methodist, which is 100 yards from our church, got the power back on just in time for church. So, they worshipped with AC, a sound system and lights, while we languished without. I teased the mayor, whose membership resides with our Methodist friends, that he must have really pulled some strings to get the power back on just in time. (I was teasing really!)

Well, I got a call last Saturday from the mayor himself because the Methodist bus had broken down (all church buses break down, it is just a matter of how often and where), and some kids and chaperones were stranded about an hour from home. They wanted to borrow our bus. I could have said, "Yes, but next time we want power too." But I restrained myself and made some calls, and soon the Methodist driver, along with the pastor, was driving the Baptist bus on a rescue mission. The Baptist bus, by the way, follows the "straight and narrow" better than the Methodist bus.

Don't you just love it when someone owes you? The mayor owes me (twice) and the wonderful folk at First Methodist are now indebted to us as well. Let's see. What would be a way to balance the scales? I think I have it. Take the pigeons back. For years the gospel birds flocked to First Methodist, and I thought they made great Methodists. But our Wesleyan friends wised up and bought some pigeon deflecting wire and put it on their steeple. Guess where the pigeons deflected? Up the street. They now have a home at our church and seem to be in no hurry to leave. Maybe our Methodist friends would want to settle up (after all, they do owe us) by taking up a "love offering" so that we poor Baptists could afford some of that fancy pigeon deflecting wire. If so, then I think the birds would make great Presbyterians.

Another solution would be to capture the pigeons, baptize them and officially make them Baptist birds. Then, we would only see them at Christmas and Easter and our problem would be solved. And the Methodists would still owe us. Or maybe the most spiritual solution would be to build a Baptist altar so that our Methodist friends down the street could come over and offer a sacrifice for their sins, "You shall bring to the Lord, as penalty for the sin that you have committed…two pigeons" (Leviticus 5:7).

Actually, we Christians believe that Christ's sacrifice is the only one we need and because of it, Baptists and Methodists stand forgiven. And we are friends who gladly loan a bus to the other and who would be happy to loan some pigeons as well.

BBQ and Babies

We had just ordered at Billy Bobs BBQ when Natalie began to act the way two-year olds can act. She was hungry and fussy. I thought she was beginning to make a scene, so I took her out to the car in the parking lot. I scolded and cuddled. I talked and listened. I wiped away tears—hers, not mine. "Now are you ready to go back into the restaurant and behave?"

Her answer was interrupted by the unmistakable sound of an overhead helicopter. I raised my head just in time to see the colors and logo on its side. I have been often to the children's hospitals in Atlanta, Eggleston and Scottish Rite, to recognize instantly that it was one of their helicopters. It had just taken off from our local hospital and was headed back to Atlanta. Its cargo? A child. Someone's child. Someone's beloved little boy or girl who was sick enough to be life-flighted to Atlanta. I don't even want to think about the horror of that. I said a little prayer for the unknown child and then looked back at mine—my healthy child.

And my attitude quickly changed from "Why can't I get mine to behave?" and "When am I going to get to go back in and eat my BBQ?" to "I'm grateful mine is healthy" and "My food can wait." Everything changed in an instant. The sight of that helicopter carrying some sick child changed the way I viewed my situation.

Mission experiences have a way of changing us. Going on a mission trip, working at the soup kitchen, or teaching a kid to read will change you as much as those to whom you minister. If we are not careful we can become isolated and insulated from the hurts of others and lose touch. If you find yourself too absorbed in your own problems, then look out and up. You just might see something that could change your life.

"And seeing the multitudes, He was moved with compassion for them, because they were lost and downcast like sheep without a shepherd" (Matthew 9:36).

Discipleship News

Teasing the Preacher

The weirdest Old Testament story is about the Prophet Elisha and his bald head. Some boys teased him, "Go away, baldhead," and the prophet wasn't amused. He "cursed them in the name of the Lord" (nice guy), and then some "she-bears" came out of the woods and mauled them (2 Kings 2: 23-24). And the moral of the story is: 1) Elisha would have made a bad children's minister; and 2) don't mess with the preacher.

Which leads me to our recent Perky Pumpkin Party (fall festival), where I sat at a table designated as the "hair painting table." Hannah Kay and Kate were the proprietors of the table and both were armed with cans of hair spray paint. So, I sat at the table knowing that the baseball hat I was wearing would cover up most of the paint no matter how bad it looked. I was their first customer of the evening, thus, I got my choice of colors. Being the Bama guy that I am, I picked red. Off came the hat and on went the paint. Lots of it. They seemed to get a certain amount of joy in unloading an entire can on my receptive head.

When they finished I had red hair all right, but wearing the cap made it tolerable. I thought that a simple shower with shampoo would take care of it, and I would be none the worse for it. It was all done in fun, and a few folk got a laugh or two out of it.

Well, I got all the paint out of my hair that night with several shampoos (about five or six), and I thought I was done. The next Wednesday I ran into the girls at church, and they pointed out that my scalp was still red. I accused them of lying. "Go look in the mirror and see." I did.

It wasn't terribly noticeable (I don't think), but pulling back the hair and looking closely, sure enough, they were right. Several days later I still had a red scalp! Then the next Sunday, same thing. Others noticed...and laughed. Two weeks later at church, "Hey Preacher Steve, you still have a red scalp," Hannah Kay said.

Kate walked by and said the same. Adults pointed and laughed, "Hey Lucy, nice hair."

I told the girls that studies have shown that if red paint stays on the scalp too long it can cause brain damage. Their response: "With you, how could we tell?" No remorse. No pity. No respect. I am the Rodney Dangerfield of the church.

When I was growing up we had one preacher that we made fun of. He had some strange things going on with his hair, and we sat in the congregation and wondered if he was intentionally trying to be out of style. I couldn't pay attention to his sermons because he had this hair thing going on. Now, I am left to wonder if my red scalp is detracting from my always scintillating sermons.

The truth is, our bantering back and forth on this has been fun. I like to dish it out to folk, so I can't complain when it comes right back at me. Teasing begets teasing. I've done my share of poking fun, and now I've just got to grin and "bear" (pardon the Elisha pun) it.

"Laughter doeth good like a medicine" (Proverbs 17:22). That is, unless of course, you laugh at Elisha. In that case, you will need more than medicine after being mauled by the bears.

Remembering Lois

I got notice this week that Lois had died. My high school classmates are passing away at an all too fast a pace. I had not talked to Lois in ages, and quite frankly, had not thought of her for a while. But the notice of her sudden death took me back to junior high days.

You see, Lois and I went "steady" for about two hours. I was the shyest kid on the block, especially around girls. I had three brothers, and all we talked about was sports. I knew more about touchdowns and fastballs than girls, and as far as I was concerned, it could stay that way forever.

And then along came Lois. She was blonde and beautiful, and one look at her, and I forgot about sports. Apparently she was fond of me. Maybe she liked my elbows and Adam's apple (it looked like I had swallowed a text book), because that's all I was. Or maybe she liked my thick, Coke bottle glasses, that reminded her of Clark Kent, aka, Superman. Or could it be that Lois liked boys who liked sports? I held out hope for all the above. All I knew was that she had a "hankerin'" for me.

And how did I know such a wondrous thing? Because her best friend, whom I had in fourth period, told me that Lois wanted to go steady with me. "Me?" I swallowed hard with that Adam's apple, and stuttered and stammered a "yes." Wow, I was going steady with Lois! Mind you, I had not yet seen Lois or talked to Lois; we had only communicated this commitment through her emissary.

Well, I then had a couple of periods to ponder what I had done. Would I actually have to carry on a conversation with her? This was uncharted territory. Would I have to kiss her? Yuck!! What would be next, no more sports? Marriage? Kids? This was too much for me. I wanted out!!

So, when sixth period rolled around, I had that same friend of Lois in that class. I emphatically told her: "I want to break up with Lois." And thus ended one of the shortest romances in history. No lawyer needed. No dividing up the property. No swapping weekends with the kids. Short and simple: "You tell Lois it is over."

Commitment was a scary thing for a little kid with pimples and Coke bottle glasses. Well, now the glasses have been replaced by contacts, the pimples have been long gone, and the shyness has been conquered. And commitments are no longer scary; I've made plenty of them since my two-hour romance with Lois.

I've made commitments to my wife, to our kids, to our church, to community organizations, and to Christ. And I don't' stutter and stammer when I make them. And I don't swallow my Adam's apple hard when I do. Commitment is what makes life go.

Following Christ is all about making a commitment. "Follow me," Jesus said to those first followers. Marriage is the same: "I do." A few simple words carry within them the power to change a life. I don't regret any of the commitments I have made.

And by the way, Lois' obituary said that she and her husband of many years had two kids. It also said that she taught the "special needs" Sunday school class at her church. I guess she learned a thing or two about commitment as well.

Sweet Home...Ethelsville?

Mom and Dad grew up in Kennedy, Alabama, a small town of about 400 in west Alabama. I know that little bit of information about them because they told me and because I have been there. The good folk of Kennedy have verified the roots there that Mom and Dad talked about. What I did not know is where Mom was born.

You see, Mom just turned 86 and so "the boys" decided it would be a good time to talk about a will, living will, roots, etc. We told Mom to write down some of the stuff about her "raising" and her siblings. In the process of doing so, Mom wrote this: "Born November 15, 1926 in Ethelsville, Alabama." When I read that I went "Huh?"

I had always assumed that Mom was born and raised in Kennedy because no one had ever told me differently. My shock turned to curiosity which led to a Google search. What I found out about my mom's home town tickled the heck out of me.

According to the 2000 census (they did not participate in the 2010 census, perhaps thinking it to be none of the government's business), the town of Ethelsville has 81 people. Of those 81, five are under 18, so there is some hope. The total area of the town is 0.6 miles. Thirty three percent of the 81 live under the poverty line.

What really cracked me up were these lines from the Wikipedia article: "The town was named after Ethel Hancock, a one time resident and staple of the community. She was famous for being Mr. Hancock's daughter."

How about that for a heritage? "Hey Ethel, what are you famous for?" What does that say about Mr. Hancock? It says he cast a wide shadow for his daughter, Ethel, to the point that a hundred or two hundred years later, she was still only known as her dad's daughter.

Expectation can be a heavy burden to carry day after day. I'm, of course just guessing, but what I'm guessing is that the pressure on young Ethel was pretty great, being "Mr. Hancock's daughter." Expectation can be a blessing or a curse, but my hunch is that for Ethel it was a blessing. When folk expect you to grow up and be something, most will actually "grow up and be something." Though high expectation can be a burden, I would gladly live with high expectations than low ones. If you grow up with folk expecting very little from you, then that is what they will probably get.

So, why is it that in the short history of that little town, she gets only scant recognition? Though a "staple of the community," she plays second fiddle to her Dad. Is it because she was a she and he was a he? Maybe in that day, as the history of that town and most towns were written, it was the males who got the headlines and credit. The females had to take a backseat in history and in practice.

Of course, when the town fathers (and mothers) got together to name their little community, they named it after her: Ethelsville. "You go girl!"

Those of us who name the name of Christ also have very high expectations placed on us. Is that a burden or a joy? How will we be remembered?

"Growing Old Ain't for Sissies"

One of my sarcastic church members (there are many) sent me an e-mail that said something like this: "When I read this, I thought about you." Well, I knew right off that it was either a corny preacher joke or an Alabama joke, given my vocation and my birth in that "land flowing with milk and honey." Well, it was neither, but the connection with me is: (1) my love of "oldies" music; and (2) my advancing years.

The header of the email said that singing artists from yesteryear are revising their lyrics to accommodate aging baby boomers. And they include such hits as Bobby Darin's "Splish, Splash, I was havin' a Flash," Herman's Hermits' "Mrs. Brown, You've got a Lovely Walker," Ringo Starr's "I Get by with a Little Help from Depends," The Bee Gees' "How Can You Mend a Broken Hip?", Paul Simon's "Fifty Ways to Lose your Liver," Leo Sayer's "You Make Me Feel Like Napping," Tony Orlando's "Knock Three Times on the Ceiling if You Hear Me Fall," Helen Ready's "I am Woman, Hear Me Snore," and my favorite, Leslie Gore's "It's My Procedure, and I'll Cry if I Want To."

Like I said, I have some sarcastic church members. Obviously I was "thought of" because I love those old songs and because I am having procedure after procedure. And though we might get a chuckle out of those revised lyrics, growing old is no laughing matter. As I have heard many of our church seniors say, "Growing old ain't for sissies."

Speaking of old, have you ever stood at the base of a giant redwood tree? I have, and they are amazing. They can reach nearly 300 feet into the air and nearly 100 feet in circumference. They are hundreds, maybe thousands, of years old. But what is more impressive is that they are still growing. They can add nearly 500 board feet per year.

As we humans age, our bodies continue to grow, just not always in the right direction or places. They typically grow in the direction of gravity. And they also grow in their rigidity and susceptibility to diseases. Growth happens without any encouragement. As long as there is life, growth never stops, even for those aging baby boomers whose lives consist of procedure after procedure.

What we need to insure is that personal, spiritual growth continues for us as we age. This can happen in lots of ways. For example, when a loved one dies or a dream dies, we need to grieve, learn, depend on God, and grow. As grandchildren come along, we need to learn from them about the simplicity of faith, about purity, innocence, (and social media). Our journey with life and with God is upward and outward. As long as we live, we should put out new leaves of faith and commitment. We should never stop growing spiritually this side of heaven.

Yes, I have a few circles around my trunk (stomach). And yes, "It's my procedure and I'll cry if I want to."

Conversations in a Holding Room

They call them holding rooms. Why holding? I think it's sort of like when an airplane circles the airport it is said to be in a holding pattern. Only this is at a hospital, and it is where the patient waits for surgery. They are small rooms, just big enough for the patient and a couple of family members, friends, or minister. I happened to be in one such room with a female patient and her close, female friend.

The conversation went something like this after the handsome doctor gave his instructions and left. "If I was going to marry again, a doctor wouldn't be a bad choice. He would have money, and he would be gone a lot. Perfect." Chuckles followed, with disclaimers that they were just kidding. I think sometimes our laughter gives us away.

Then the family's deacon came into the holding room for a visit. He stayed for a minute or two and then led in a prayer. Perfect. Well, almost. Wouldn't you know it, right in the middle of his prayer, my dad gum cell phone went off. One of my many pet peeves is cell phones going off at the wrong time. The wrong time is any time that I deem inappropriate. During church would be one such time! I have heard them during weddings and funerals, and my blood boils. Some golfers talk on their cell phones the entire time they are on the course. What's the point in playing?

Well, lo and behold, this time it was mine. Not only did it go off, but it played a song which my son picked out for me last time he was home. I love James Taylor and so my ring tone is now his "Shower the People." Sing it with me:

> Shower the people you love with love.
> Show them the way that you feel.
> Things are gonna work out fine if you only will.
> Shower the people you love with love.
> Show them the way that you feel.
> Things are gonna be much better if you only will.

Those aren't bad words, by the way, for a preacher's phone and not bad words for a holding room. Well, not only did James begin crooning in the middle of the deacon's prayer, it was on high volume, so everyone in Tanner Hospital heard it. Folks in comas heard it. Patients under heavy anesthesia heard it, I am sure. And to make matters worse, the phone was in the pocket of my heavy winter coat, and brother James sang about three verses before I could silence him.

Prayer is a sacred conversation with God, whether in a prayer room or a holding room. I am amused at all the political debate about public prayers, when in fact, Jesus never said a good word about them, noting that hypocrites like public prayers because they can be heard by others (Matthew 6:5). Rather, He said, when you pray go to your closet and pray (v.6). Pray to God, not others. Given the size of the holding room, that was as close to a closet prayer as you will find.

I'm sorry that my cell phone interrupted a beautiful prayer from a deacon and ruined a sacred moment. The next time someone's phone goes off during worship I will be less judgmental. But maybe at least it will be a ring tone I like. And "Shower the People" would work very nicely in the sanctuary.

"Stir Crazy"

What do you call it? Stir Crazy? Cabin Fever? Whatever you call it, I had it. I had it during a recent snow/ice event. They say that you can tell you have it because you become irritable. Sheri said that with me, how could she tell. Anyway, after a couple of cooped up days, I was going nuts. Sheri thought that our dog might be in danger from my right foot. I was afraid that I might start throwing things, like plates and insults. The final straw was when I started banging my head against the wall for no apparent reason. Sheri said (with tenderness, of course), "Get out."

So, I left and went to work, and I just happened to have my phone on silence. So, for about two or three hours I had no contact from the outside world. Lucky for me, as it would turn out. What I didn't know was that during that time out of the house Sheri had desperately tried to reach me. She had tried to reach me because our basement flooded due to a malfunction of our now-defunct water heater. The Davis clan is a resourceful bunch. We just opened the windows and doors, and with below freezing temps, we turned the basement into an ice-skating rink. (OK, I made that part up.)

By the time I got home to help deal with the crisis, we already had a company pumping water out of the basement. They came quickly because a friend has a relative who worked for them who called a friend, who called another friend, etc. In addition, by the time I got home, we had a friend's dad at the house because he knows how to install new water heaters. I have no clue about such things. So, he and I went to the hardware store to buy a water heater with a friend's parent, while, back at the ranch, a friend of a relative was pumping H$_2$O out of our soggy basement. Get the point?

If not for friends our basement would still resemble the Atlanta Aquarium. I don't know what in the world I would do without friends. A survey of 1,500 American adults revealed that nearly 25% of them said they had zero close friends, persons with whom they could discuss personal matters. How sad.

General William Westmoreland, during the Vietnam War, was reviewing a platoon of paratroopers. As he went down the line, he asked each of them a question: "How do you like jumping, son?" "Love it sir," was the first answer. "How do you like jumping?" he asked the second. "The greatest experience of my life!" exclaimed the paratrooper. "How do you like jumping?" he asked the third. "I hate it sir!" he replied. "Then why do you do it?" asked Westmoreland. "Because I love being with these guys who love jumping, sir." Now that is friendship. Is there someone in your life with whom you are that close? Do you have a friend whose sentences you can finish?

"Two are better than one, because they have a good reward for their toil. For if they fall, one will lift up the other; but woe to one who is alone and falls and does not have another to help" (Ecclesiastes 4:9-10). I would add, "Woe to him whose basement floods and there is no friend to call."

"Hello" to the 21st Century

It is like having a new bike under the Christmas tree but not knowing how to ride it. You think, "If someone will just show me how, I'm really going to enjoy taking it for a ride." Or you think, "Well, I'll learn by trial and error, and I may fall off a few times, but eventually I'll get it."

So, what do I have that is like that? I have a new iPhone, and quite frankly, I don't know what to do with it. It looks pretty, like a new bike under the tree, and I'm sure once I am using it, I will be thrilled by it. But it may take awhile. You see, apparently, if you can remember The Ed Sullivan Show, then you can't easily learn how to operate an iPhone. If you owned a 45 RPM record of Elvis singing "Hound Dog," then operating an iPhone won't come naturally. I am on the wrong side of the great time divide. I didn't grow up with this technology, and though it doesn't scare me, and though I am trying to embrace it, I don't get along well with it.

So, for a couple of days my new toy lay on my desk, and I just stared at it. I didn't know if it just automatically came on by itself, or if it would talk back to me. After a few days, I discovered the

"On" button and off we went. Before too long I could actually make and receive phone calls on it. Imagine that. Before the turn of this year's calendar, I hope to be able to check emails, use the internet, and operate the camera on it. Maybe that is wishful thinking.

Incidentally, I had to say goodbye to an old friend, my monthly calendar, the Day-Timer. I have had Day-Timer as my pocket companion for some 25 years, and our parting was not easy. It was a painful divorce. She had outlived her usefulness to me, and yet parting with her was like a breakup of Barney and Thelma Lou (sorry for the peek into the past). I had grown quite comfortable with her, and she had kept me punctual for most of my calendar events since '85, when we were first introduced. But it was time. It was time to move into the 21st century. I also, by the way, sold my carrier pigeon and started using email.

So, goodbye Day-Timer, hello iPhone. It is supposed to make my life easier, by the way, and my work more efficient. Time will tell. I do know that it is a whole lot more fun, with all its bells and whistles, than a Day-Timer. And my seven-year-old can do more on it than I can.

I refuse to live my life in the past and talk about the "good ole days." I refuse to be afraid of modern things just because they are different. Will Rogers once said, "Things ain't what they used to be and probably never were." I don't idolize the past, nor do I overdose on nostalgia. I don't believe for one minute that all of the good things happened in the past, nor do I think that God did His best work in the past. Someone said that there's one thing God won't do, and that is an encore. I happen to believe that God is not behind us but rather, out in front of us, leading us into a bright future.

"Eye hath not seen, nor ear heard, nor the human heart conceived, what God has prepared for those who love Him" (1 Corinthians 2:9).

My only problem with the iPhone is worry that I might misplace it. That happened last year with my eight-track player.

"What Happens at Steak'n Shake Stays at..."

I have only been to Vegas one time, and on that one occasion, my wife went with me. I know from the saying, "What happens in Vegas stays in Vegas," that you can "act a fool" if you want in Vegas, and no one back home will know. If you go there alone, then I suppose you can gamble, fool around, etc., and the tales of your exploits won't be whispered beyond the Vegas city limits.

The old saying goes like this: "Character is how you act when no one else is around." Some folk have gone to Vegas alone or on a "business trip" and their true character has gone on display. All of which brings me to Steak'n Shake.

My wife was out of town on a Friday evening, and Natalie was spending the night with a friend. "Hot diggity dog, a night all to myself." I have a confession: I went to Steak'n Shake and got a burger, fries, and a delicious chocolate milk shake the size of a blackjack table. For some reason, I felt guilty going there. I snuck in like a Baptist at a liquor store, took a seat at the counter, and hoped no one would see me and send a picture to Sheri. The headline would read: "Local Baptist minister caught stuffing his face on Friday night eating spree."

The Friday night guilt came as a result of reading an article in the Friday morning paper. The article noted a study about Southerners' high rate of strokes because of our high rate of consuming fried food. Having digested that info in the AM, I knew that my Friday PM choice of food should have been a salad or a veggie plate. But the saying is true about character coming out when you are alone.

I know what to do but don't always do it. I know what to eat and what not to eat, but I don't always make good choices. I am more likely to make good choices when I have good folk around me (can you say wife?) to hold me accountable, but when I don't, watch out.

The Apostle Paul had his share of temptations, but Steak'n Shake was not one of them. He lamented (Romans 7) the fact that he knew he should do good, and he knew right from wrong, but even the great Christian leader himself struggled to make good choices. He did not always "eat his veggies," if you know what I mean.

Food temptations (shakes, chocolate, etc.) are significant, but we should expand the discussion. Let's talk real temptation. Jesus was really tempted. Some folk are bothered by that, but He was. If you read His temptations in Matthew 4: 1-11, then we are not in the baby pool anymore. We are wading in the deep water.

A man sits in his room shaking. He's got a bad case of the shakes (not milk shakes). Two days without a drink of liquor. He tells his friends, "I'll never drink again. I've almost lost my family; I have already lost my job." His wife is in the kitchen crying and his kids are in the bedroom trembling. You see, they know what daddy is like when he is drinking. What he knows, that they don't, is that there is a half pint of liquor stored in a cabinet. When everybody leaves…well, now we are talking real temptation.

That's tough, really tough. Confess your weakness. Ask God for strength. And when the wife is out of town, make good choices. Order the salad.

Hallie Gets It Right

Hallie is a really cute little girl in our church, and she gets it. After her recent baptism, she made a card for me. On one side of the card she colored a black heart. When she first gave it to me I thought it odd—a black heart. (Maybe she knows me better than I think.) Then I turned the card over and on the other side she had colored a beautiful red, orange, and yellow heart with the words: "Thank you for baptizing me. I am happy that I am baptized."

Leave it to a child to speak the complicated truth in simple terms and with simple art. All of us have a dark heart and a colorful heart. Even the great Apostle Paul spoke of his sin, "For what I am doing, I do not understand; for I am not practicing what I would like to do, but I am doing the very thing that I hate" (Romans 7).

Paul was the original Dr. Jekyll and Mr. Hyde. The book by Robert Louis Stevenson is about a Dr. Jekyll, who was a good, moral man raised in Victorian England with a strict sense of right and wrong, but who had a dark side, Mr. Hyde. Dr. Jekyll was tormented by evil impulses that he sometimes secretly indulged. And he couldn't be happy as a good man because of these evil impulses, but he couldn't be happy as an evil man because of his conscience. As the plot thickened he tried a chemical solution to his problem, which sounds a lot like modern day America. Well, Dr. Jekyll's experiment failed, and he lost control of when he would be Dr. Jekyll and when he would be Mr. Hyde.

Stevenson's book is not the end of the story. "The Good Book" has more to say about the subject. The Bible offers the painfully honest, but good news, which is that every sinner has a future and every saint has a past. Paul had a past, a bad past. He also had a bright future.

Another great example from the Bible is that of Simon Peter, who plays such a prominent role in the Holy Week story. He had a wonderful nickname, by the way. Do any of you have one? I had a horrible nickname growing up: "Wormy." I got it because of my awesome build. I was so skinny I only had one stripe on my pajamas. Now that's skinny. I know the guy who gave the nickname to me and to this day, his picture is on my dart board. I hope that in the next life he pays for giving me such a horrible nickname.

Simon Peter had a nickname, a good one: "Rock." Guess who gave it to him? Jesus. This is the Simon Peter, who in the gospel accounts is proud, boastful, and impetuous. This is the same Simon Peter who out of anger, cut off a man's ear. It was this Simon Peter who would deny Jesus three times like a coward and then run for his life. Simon had a dark side. Simon was Dr. Jekyll one day and Mr. Hyde the next. One day he was a rock and the next day, a coward.

But Jesus knew the good and bad in Peter and offered him grace. Jesus said you can call this man "Rock." Jesus offered him grace and made a changed man out of him.

Someone said, "Treat a man as he is and he will remain as he is. Treat a man as he can and should be and he will become what he can and should be." The truth is, all of us are two persons. We are the person we are, and we are the person we can become.

Hallie, thanks so much for the card and for the reminder.

The Parable of Joe and His Dog

Fact: Joe McGinnis, long-time, former Carrollton mayor, is a better man than I. Those of you who know both of us don't need proof. Others might. The proof is in our canine friends. Joe has a dog named Mikey, a three-legged, miniature Dachshund. Joe loves his dog more than I do mine. His beloved Mikey disappeared for several days. Short of an organized dog hunt led by Mayor Garner and Police Chief Richards, Joe did everything he could to find his beloved pet.

The tale (wagging tail) has a happy ending. Mikey was next door at the neighbors, disoriented, and trapped under the neighbor's house.

Now to the part about Joe being a better man. He is a better man because of what he said. I could tell that he meant what he said. Some of us run our mouths and don't mean it. Joe meant it. The "it" that he meant was these words: "I would not take a million dollars for my dog." Before I could drop my jaw, he said it again.

My dog is not for sale, but if she were, the asking price would be a lot lower. If someone offered me a million dollars for my dog, you can't imagine how fast I would run to the bank. We have a good dog, but sometimes she drives me nuts. (Sheri says, in golf terms, it is not a drive, but a putt.)

I am not very emotionally attached to our dog, certainly not a million dollars' worth of emotion. Joe told me that once a person gets older, and the kids are grown up, you tend to form a bond with your pets. I'm "older" but all the kids are not grown, and I am definitely not there with the bonding thing and our dog.

Jesus told three stories about losing things that are valuable. A shepherd lost his beloved sheep, a woman lost a coin, and a father lost a (prodigal) son. I suppose that, out of those three stories, Mickey is more like the lost sheep—he did not intend to get lost; it just happened. Sheep, like dogs, get lost and wind up under the neighbor's house, disoriented and trapped.

I know people who get lost, disoriented, and trapped, but they did not set out with that in mind. Ask anyone with an addiction to drugs or alcohol if they intended for life to wind up like this. Have you ever known someone to say, "When I grow up I want to be an alcoholic; I want to lose my job, family, and friends." One thing, one bad choice leads to another, and they wind up in a bad way, in a bad place in life.

The purpose of the three stories Jesus told was that God is like the shepherd, the woman, and the father. God really cares when something valuable, like you and me, is lost. He goes to great lengths to find what is lost.

If Jesus had lived in Carrollton, GA he would have told a fourth story, the one about a man named Joe who lost his dog and searched until he found him. Unknown to Joe, his beloved Mikey was next door the whole time. That story is like all the lost people I know; so close to God and they don't even know it.

Did I just say that Joe McGinnis is like God? OK, sorry. He is a better person than I, but not that much better.

Monday Morning Homily

Hanging out with Dad is not her favorite thing to do, especially on the first official day of summer. You see, my wife is a teacher and has what they call post-planning for a few days after school is out. And thus, our then eight-year-old had to hang out with Dad. Hanging out with me meant going with me to work and finding something meaningful to do for most of the day.

She has spent much time in my office, and she actually has some colors, paper, etc. stored under my desk. She has a small lamp as well, and she is quite capable of making good use of her time while I work. But on this day, that would not do. Perhaps, graduation to the third grade had changed her. On that day, she wanted no part of going to work with me or of coloring or reading for several hours.

As we left the house, she grabbed our son, Tyler's, iPod Touch. Hopefully, that would be enough to scratch her entertainment itch. An eight-year-old can't be satisfied with mere books and colors; no she has to have the latest stuff. As we walked up the church sidewalk, she was holding the iPod in her tiny hand. They don't give those gadgets away. I had this sinking feeling that she would drop it on the concrete, damage it, and the world as we know it might end.

All I said was, "Don't drop Tyler's iPod." What she said was truer than anything I have ever uttered from any pulpit. She said, "Dad, you worry about things that probably aren't going to happen."

She was right. I don't normally receive sermons; I give them. And I certainly don't get them on Monday morning. But I got one—right between the eyes.

I do worry too much about stuff that probably won't happen. Author Charles Poole tells the story about when he was about eight-years-old and his family went to see his granddad, Daddy Gene.[4] One summer, he was sitting on the front porch of Daddy Gene and Ma Bessie's house in Kite, Georgia. There was a big open field across the road from their house. That evening a dark cloud, a storm cloud covered the horizon like a blanket. He remembers watching forks of lightning dart from the clouds to the earth. He was scared, almost to death.

He kept thinking that any moment Daddy Gene would say, "We'd better go on in the house." Finally, scared Charles blurted out, "Daddy Gene, don't you 'spect we'd better go inside before that storm comes?" For some strange reason, he remembers to this day that old man's red-skinned hand on his little eight-year-old knee. And then in that slow rhythm of his sharecropper's voice, Daddy Gene said, "Don't worry about that storm boy. It's goin' to go around. That lightning is a far piece from here."

---

[4] Poole, *Don't Cry Past Tuesday,* 15.

What Daddy Gene said about those clouds on that day is true about most clouds on most of our days. Most of the storms we fear never come any way. Worrying about them changes nothing. The lightning is far away, and the storm that scares us rarely strikes us.

And by the way, Tyler's iPod didn't get dropped, and the world didn't end.

Paul said, "Be anxious for nothing..." (Philippians 4:6). Good advice, but I'll bet Paul didn't have kids and iPods.

"Got Milk?"

I knew what Sheri meant when she said, "Honey, we are out of milk." Given that we are a milk loving family—drinking it, putting it on cereal and in coffee—I knew what she meant. Since it was about 9:00 at night, what she meant was, "Will you go and get some milk?" And being the dutiful husband that I am, I said "yes," though with some grumbling about her unfulfilled promise to go to the grocery store that day.

I have made these late night runs before, and I always have the same dilemma. Since we don't live very close to a grocery store, do I drive across town and pay less or go to a closer gas station and pay more? Given the late night hour and coupled with some laziness, I opted for the gas station milk and the higher prices. Higher? When I got to the register to pay, I thought the clerk misunderstood. I didn't want to buy a cow; I just wanted some of the cow's milk. Let's just say it cost, for a gallon of milk, more than a gallon of gas.

So I posed the question to the clerk. I asked her, as if it was her fault, why we could drill for oil half way around the world, process that oil, and ship it to that gas station for less than the price of milk? This particular brand of milk, by the way, was the only kind that station had. I looked on the container to see where it was made. It is processed (pasteurized or whatever you do to milk to make it drinkable) right here in Georgia, with Georgia cows, I assume.

Do you ever feel like you are being ripped off? "Hey, something is not right here." It's a bad feeling when we think we have been the victim of an injustice. It happens a lot on a much grander scale than a late night run for milk.

I have read, as have you, about people who have been vindicated by DNA evidence after spending years in jail for a crime they didn't commit. What an unthinkable injustice. While their kids are growing up, they are growing old in prison. While their kids are having birthday parties, they are having "pity parties." They rot in a jail cell for a crime they didn't commit. Injustices happen every day in our community, country, and world. And as Christians, we should care deeply about that.

One of the great themes of the Old and New Testaments is justice. If you want to be made uneasy about your affluent life, then read Amos from the Old Testament. As he denounced the affluence of his day and the hypocrisy of religious people, he then preached those now famous words, "Let justice roll down like waters" (Amos 5:24).

I know our justice system isn't perfect, but I haven't ever heard of a better one. There are a lot of good people in it. And yet we all know that justice is not distributed equally. Many poor people can't afford an attorney, much less a good one. As someone said, "Better to be rich and guilty than innocent and poor." I think that is true some of the time. Some of the time is too much of the time.

I think justice for all is a Christian theme that isn't talked about nearly enough. And I should care about it every day, not just when we are out of milk.

Galileo and Me

When you are married to a school teacher the car becomes the classroom. So, with our eight-year-old daughter in the backseat and Sheri in the front, we drive and talk about multiplication tables. With a minister driving, the conversation occasionally turns to communion tables. But mostly it is school stuff.

I don't remember what prompted this, but our daughter blurted out that she knows four planets. "What are the four that you know?" we asked. Natalie then listed them, in no particular order: "Mars, Earth, Mercury, and Leviticus." Only a preacher's kid would confuse the Old Testament book Leviticus with Venus.

We laughed with her, but it was an honest mistake for a kid who has learned her books of the Bible and who is learning the planets. Truth is, there is a lot about the Bible and science that I don't understand.

Her response got me to thinking that those two (religion and science) really should not be enemies or strange bed-fellows. I am reminded of Galileo, the 17th century Italian mathematician, astronomer, and premier scientist. He was the first to use a telescope, and his observations forced him to side with Copernicus, who a century before, had concluded that the earth was not the immovable center of the universe. For that, Galileo was investigated by the Roman inquisition of 1633. After all, the scriptures declare: "God fixed the earth upon its foundation, not to be moved forever" (Psalm 104:5).

Galileo was one smart dude. So, after viewing the instruments of torture in that day, he decided it best to repent of his scientific conclusions. As a concession, church officials spared his life, but he spent his last eight years under house arrest. For what? For believing what we take as fact today. And for daring to believe something that contradicted an established (but wrong) interpretation of scripture.

In 1992, the Roman Catholic Church admitted that Galileo was innocent of heresy and that he was scientifically correct. There are some conclusions that we Christians (Baptists have been as guilty as our Catholic friends) can draw from that experience:

- we should not idolize our interpretation of scripture;
- we don't honor the Bible when we shield it from truth;
- we don't honor God by refusing to admit our human limitations;
- we can't discover truth by canonizing our ignorance.

To keep on learning in life we must have a reverence for this mysterious universe. I am pretty much in awe of Mother Nature. I'm also in awe of God. And I don't pretend to know or understand either fully.

By the way, I know all the books of the Bible and all the planets in order. But it's really easy to get them confused. If Pluto is not an Old Testament prophet, he should be.

Sweet Home

I am a true Alabamian. For example, I think that deer season is a national holiday. I only know four spices: salt, pepper, ketchup, and Tabasco. For me, vacation is going to a family reunion. I measure distance in minutes. I also use "fix" as a verb, as in "I am fixing to go to the store."

A few years ago, a devastating tornado ripped through Tuscaloosa, and I went there to take some tornado relief supplies, and to see first-hand the damage. And I now have a new use of "fix," as in, "There is a lot that needs to be fixed." Lynyrd Skynyrd got it wrong when they sang "Sweet Home Alabama, where the skies are so blue." On one terrible Wednesday in April of 2011 the skies turned from blue to a menacing gray.

You have heard it said, "Pictures don't do it justice." It's true. I had seen pictures of the devastation, but I was taken aback seeing it firsthand. It looked like bombs had been dropped all over the city. Where once there were stores and homes, there is now rubble. I saw what was once a brand new, beautiful school, and all that was left was the sign that read, elementary school. I couldn't recognize what used to be a Krispy Kreme, one of my favorite hang outs.

I hate tornadoes. I hate them for the fear they bring. (My niece, who was then a student at the University of Alabama, was in a closet as the storm blew out windows in her apartment and killed people across the street.) I hate them because of all the heartache they caused all over the South that terrible day. I hate them because whenever they show up, there is a lot of stuff that needs fixin.'

I also hate tornadoes because they are so mean. Do you think that tornadoes have personalities? Think about it. In those minutes that they exist, do they become like people, with minds, wills, and personalities? How else can you explain the trail they leave that needs fixin'? What else but meanness would cause those angry winds to sniff out trailer parks? Why do they seem to unleash their fury on the poorest of the poor? That's what I thought as I toured Tuscaloosa and looked at what used to be Alberta City and Holt, areas of that city that were not as well-to-do as others. What a mean storm. What fury. I hate tornadoes.

I am glad to report that lots of fixin' is going on there. Volunteers from that other school (Auburn) and some foreign lands (like Louisiana) have pitched in to help. We fight back at these storms by learning lessons. One such lesson is that if we are going to fix any of our world's problems, it will take lots of working together and hand holding. I am grateful that out of life's storms, in spite of all the heartache they bring, lots of good comes. Donations pour in from all over, volunteers from Timbuktu show up with trucks, shovels, and toilet tissue. Fans from Bama, Auburn, and LSU work side by side helping hurting folk. It's a beautiful sight.

As we say in Alabama, "Who'da thunk it?"

"I Love Baseball More Than..."

Tommy Lasorda was, for many years, manager of the Los Angeles Dodgers and a Hall of Fame manager as well. He has always been a funny guy who shined when the camera was on him. He has lived and breathed baseball for all of his life. Lasorda has been married to the same woman, Jo, for 61 years.

A few years ago, he had to leave home for a speaking engagement in Chattanooga with the Dodgers' minor league team, the Lookouts. So, once again he had to tell his wife goodbye and board a plane for something related to baseball. As he left, his wife said to him, "I have finally figured it out. You love baseball more than me." To which the quick-witted Lasorda responded, "Yes, but I love you more than football and basketball."

Actually I love all three (and throw in golf as well), but I don't love them more than I love my wife. It is true that I spend more time staring at the TV watching the Braves than I do in meaningful conversation with her. It is also true that I can spend four hours on the golf course and love it, but four hours on the couch talking about how the day went would send me to the funny farm. But I do love her more, just in a different way.

My love of the Braves is getting out of hand. Did you watch the recent 19 inning game with the Pirates? Raise your hand if you stayed up and watched all of it. I did, almost. I kept saying, "One more inning. Just one more." I went to sleep after the 17th (about 1:00 AM), not able to hold the eyes open any longer. And so I missed the Braves' win on a very controversial call by the home plate umpire.

Was it an exciting game until that last inning? No, in fact, watching it was like staring at pond water. There was more excitement in a C-Span rerun. But for some reason, I hung in there with the local team as they battled the Pirates for one game out of a 162 game season.

The next day at work, I was bleary-eyed and had the attention span of a five-year-old. Why? Do I love baseball that much? Are my priorities way out of whack? Am I so competitive that I can't let go of a close game? How about all of the above?

We all do stupid stuff and afterwards say, "What was I thinking?" We get caught up in the moment and lose perspective. That has happened to many a teenager in the back seat of a Ford. Or, our emotions about a game get the best of us and we throw reason and decency out the window. That has happened to lots of parents at their kid's baseball game. Emotion trumps reason. The wise person thinks before doing something stupid. The writer of Proverbs says that when wisdom enters your heart "discretion shall guard you and understanding will watch over you" (2:10-11).

Having said that, I still can't fully explain why I spent about six hours on the couch watching a baseball game when my body and mind needed rest. My church should dock my pay for showing up at work with a brain that was as pooped as the Braves' players the next day. I am making a commitment not to do that again—at least until the playoffs!

Tide for Toomers

Admitting that I am a die-hard Alabama fan may cost me some readers, but given the fact that only Bama fans can read, I'm OK. (I couldn't resist.) I was a Bama fan before I was born. I had no choice, not if I wanted hot meals and a bed at night. All my parents' families are from the Tuscaloosa area, and my Mom and Dad and three brothers went to the U of A. At my Aunt Ruby's funeral in Tuscaloosa, the preacher said that she loved three things: God, family, and Alabama football. I don't doubt that for one minute, but I think he got the order wrong. I have a first cousin who was Bear Bryant's personal driver for 10 years, and if you think I am making that up, I will give you Mom's number for verification.

I was eaten up with it since a kid. Once when we got some new neighbors, Mom said, "They are nice, but they are Auburn." It was like they had some dreaded disease, and maybe we should put their names on the prayer list at church or pray for an exorcism. And by the way, I try to make sure that we sing the hymn "Grace Greater than our Sin" at least once a week at our church, because the third stanza goes like this, "Dark is the stain that we cannot hide, What can avail to wash it away? Look! There is flowing a **crimson tide**…"

All of which leads me to the raging news story about the Alabama fan, Harvey Almorn Updyke, age 62, who allegedly poisoned the famed 130-year oak trees on Toomer's Corner in Auburn. Auburn has a tradition that after winning football games, the oak trees are covered in toilet tissue. We Alabama fans have never understood all the hoop de doo about toilet tissue in trees, but for Auburn fans it is a sacred thing. All universities have some traditions that outsiders just don't get. For example, don't mess with the hedges in Athens, GA. Other schools have hedges around their football field, but to Dawg fans, their hedges are sacred. Poisoning the trees at Toomer's Corner would be akin to burning those hedges, I suppose.

Well, let's get this out of the way: Harvey Updyke is a nut. He named his son Bear and his daughter Crimson. (We have a son and daughter, and I am wondering why I didn't think of that first.) Mr. Updyke needs two things: a good lawyer and an even better therapist. If convicted, he could spend many years in prison, where I'm guessing that one of his punishments will be no watching of Bama games on Saturday. That might just do him in.

College football in the South has gotten out of hand, and some fans have gone way over the top. I still love it, but the older I get, the more I realize that other things are more important. When grown men and women's self-esteem is wrapped up in how 19-year-olds play on Saturday, then something is amiss.

Sometimes bad things lead to good things. The Apostle Paul thought so because he said that "all things work together for good…" (Romans 8:28). Because of Mr. Updyke's foolishness, fans of college football will take a deep breath and reflect on the role of sports in their lives. Maybe fans from both sides will sit down together at the same table and talk…and be friends. Some Bama fans have started a Facebook page called "Tide for Toomers," where they are raising money for the saving of the trees.

I hope the trees can be saved. Though I don't understand it, rolling the trees is a nice tradition, except when they beat Bama. Then it stinks.

Half Time Blunder

We all make mistakes. But hers was a doozie. Hers was before "God and everybody." My mistakes are usually noticed by family, say when I lose my temper or leave my socks where socks aren't to be left. Church members hear my mistakes when I say the wrong thing in a sermon, such as "The Lord is a shoving leopard" or in a wedding when I say, "It is kisstomary to cuss the bride." It happens.

I'm glad that I am not Christina Aguilera, who botched the "Star Spangled Banner' at halftime of a Super Bowl. Everybody saw it live, has seen a replay on YouTube or has read about it. What did she do that was so bad? She messed up the words. I think she got her "rocket's red glare" mixed up with her "ramparts we watched." Who hasn't? I've blown the words singing it in the shower. OK, I don't actually sing the National Anthem in the shower, but if I did, I would. People are giving her a little slack because our national anthem is hard to sing, and the words are a bit awkward.

Some have suggested over the years that we change our national anthem to something easier to sing and remember, like say, "America the Beautiful.' I would vote for that. Actually, I think it should be "Sweet Home Alabama," perhaps the greatest song and anthem ever written.

When mistakes are made, there comes the possibility of redemption. Aguilera is getting calls from around the country to sing the anthem to make amends. A New York Mets' minor league team, the Brooklyn Cyclones, has asked her to sing it this summer. If she blows it again, I don't think she will find minor league baseball fans as forgiving as Super Bowl fans.

In 1906 a man named Elmer Beehler invented the backspace on a typewriter. (A typewriter was an ancient writing device used last century.) The backspace allowed the user to redo a mistake. Since none of us type perfectly or live perfectly (or sing perfectly for that matter), we could all use a backspace. A do-over. In golf they are called mulligans. When a golfer hits a bad shot, he may in some amateur settings, take another shot—a second chance.

I've had lots of mulligans in life. I have worn out the backspace. There is nothing more significant or foundational to our faith than the opportunity for forgiveness and a second chance. Do you remember that Simon Peter denied Jesus three times? He blew it big time. But after Jesus' resurrection, the angel said to the women at the tomb, "Go and tell His disciples and Peter..." He had been singled out to hear about the resurrection. That was his chance for a mulligan.

Christina Aguilera needs a do-over. I say we give it to her.

"Boogity, Boogity, Boogity?"

I have never met the Rev. Joe Nelms, but I would like to. And if I did, I would like to ask him if he has any clue as to the difference between public and private prayer. The reason I would like to ask him is because of the very public prayer he offered at the NASCAR Nationwide Federated Auto Parts 300 in 2011. In his "prayer," he thanked God for Dodges, Toyotas, and Fords, for GM performance technology, and for RO7 engines (whatever they are). And borrowing a line from the movie, "Talladega Nights," and Will Ferrell (never borrow from Will Ferrell when offering a prayer), he thanked God for his "smokin' hot wife." He concluded his prayer with, "In Jesus' name, boogity, boogity, boogity, Amen."

He got lots of laughs, which I am sure he wanted, and his 15 minutes of fame, which regrettably lasted several weeks. He obviously knew his audience and prayed to them (I'm sorry but I couldn't help it). Prayer is a sacred conversation with God.

And now back to the question of does Rev. Nelms know the difference between public and private prayers? Jesus never said anything good about public prayers, by the way. He said, in fact, that hypocrites like to pray in public (synagogues and street corners) where they will be seen and heard by men (Matthew 5:5). Do 100,000 people at a NASCAR event qualify? I'm guessing that Jesus had in mind prayers at Daytona and Talladega when he said that. Conversely, Jesus said that when we pray we should go to our closets, shut the door, and God will hear us in private (6:6). Jesus also said, "Don't heap up empty phrases like the Gentiles" (6:7). Wouldn't "boogity, boogity, boogity" qualify as an empty phrase?

There has been a lot of discussion about public prayers in our country in recent years. Those making the argument for public prayers apparently don't care what Jesus said about the matter. I was once asked to say a prayer at a high school football game. I stopped people with mouths full of popcorn, with cheerleaders in mid-jump, and players and coaches in mid-snarl at the opponents and said, "Let us pray." If I am ever asked to do that again, I will politely decline. It was the most irreverent prayer I have ever offered. And it definitely wasn't in a closet, unless you consider a press box to be one.

We do offer public prayers at church, but it seems to me, that is different. At church, we have in fact, come together to pray. We want to pray. We expect someone to lead us in a prayer. Public praying at church is difficult as well, as we talk to God with a few hundred people eavesdropping on our conversation. Ask anyone with white knuckles who has grabbed the pulpit and stuttered and stammered a "Let us pray." It's tough.

If Rev. Nelms wants to thank God for his "smokin' hot wife" then he should do that in private, not public. (If I ever do that to my wife, I will be the one in need of prayer.) And show a little respect for prayer and for our faith and leave out the "boogity, boogity, boogity" stuff.

And one more thing, why oh why, does he have to be a Baptist minister?

Eye See You

About my fourth grade year, I came home from school and said, "Mom, I can't see the board." For that matter, I couldn't see baseballs or girls, but I thought I could get her attention if I tied it to education. Thus, my optic odyssey began. We made an appointment to see Dr. Denny, the local optometrist. There was a bunch of letters on a chart, with an E about the size of a slab of ribs. "Steve, can you read the letters?" "What letters?" I asked. "The letters on the chart?" he said. "What chart?" I stammered. (Are you beginning to see a pattern here?) "The chart on the wall?" he said. Okay, you fill in the blank. "What ____?" I exaggerate a tad, but I couldn't see diddlysquat.

I needed glasses in the worst sort of way. And I got them alright. Coke bottle in nature. I looked like Clark Kent without the muscles and cape. My glasses looked like a pair of binoculars attached to my face with a bungee cord. Even though I could now see, I looked like a dork. I could see the board, but it came with such a heavy price. Glasses back in those days were ugly. You didn't get to pick out a pretty frame with your favorite color. We were told that our glasses would be in our new favorite color—black. They came in one color, and they all looked alike—ugly as sin.

In junior high, I threw away my glasses for hard contact lenses. Hallelujah, I had a social life after years of exile. But alas, they too came with a price. Every time the wind blew, it would hurl chunks of dirt and dust into my eyes, and I would have tears the size of Frisbees running down (and dodging zits) on my face. So much for the social life. Hard contact lenses may have let us throw away our glasses, but they came with their own headaches—cleaning, storing, popping out in the middle of gym class, and eye irritation. Over the years, I have worn every type of contact lens on the market.

In recent years, I have had to resort to reading glasses. I own about twenty pair that I keep everywhere but where I am when I need them. They are kind of like umbrellas. You own several, but never have one when you need it. And with the reading glasses, those childhood taunts of "four eyes" have turned into "six eyes." (two for natural eyes; two for contacts; two for reading glasses.) Those deacons can be rough on a pastor.

Several years ago, I decided that enough was enough, and I had Lasik surgery. It worked great and now the deacons don't taunt me, and my social life is back. Modern medicine is so incredible, but I wonder how much we take it for granted. I think about all the little children in this world who have poor eyesight because of a vitamin deficiency, but who will never have Lasik surgery, much less contacts or glasses.

Jesus said that God sent Him to "proclaim release to the captives, and that the blind will see" (Luke 4:18). If that was central to the work of Christ, then it should be central to our work as well. I can't heal blindness, but I can support the mission efforts in our community that provide glasses and vision screenings for the poor. Let's not turn a blind eye to those in need. "What letters? What chart? What wall? What poor?"

"I Can't Get No Respect"

I loved the late comedian, Rodney Dangerfield, and his weird sense of humor. He was known for yanking on his tie and saying, "I tell you, I can't get no respect." (English teachers hated his grammar.) And then he would launch into a joke or a one-liner to illustrate his lack of respect. For example, "I tell you, I can't get no respect. My father carries around the picture of the kid who came with his wallet. I tell you, I can't get no respect. Once when I was lost I saw a policeman and asked him to help me find my parents. I said to him, 'Do you think we will ever find them?' He said, 'I don't know kid. There are so many places they could hide.'" I could go on and on with his stuff.

Our family was eating recently at Evergreen's Chinese, and that is where I started feeling like Rodney Dangerfield. As you know, it is a custom in American Chinese restaurants that each customer gets a fortune cookie. I understand that in China, they don't do fortune cookies. Anyway, Sheri opened hers: "Don't worry about the stock market. Invest in family." Good advice. Then Natalie opened hers: "You will soon bring joy to someone." I thought, "Yes she can by going home and going to sleep without fussing." Then I opened mine and ...there was no message inside my cookie. Have you ever heard of an empty fortune cookie? "I tell you I can't get no respect."

The truth is, I don't rely on fortune cookies to help determine my fate or to help me make decisions. If I were going that route, then I might as well consult horoscopes or a crystal ball. People ask me from time to time, "How do I know God's will for my life?" I say, "Have you tried 'Ini mini miny moe'?" Okay, what I really say in response to that question is, "Do God's will today, and tomorrow will take care of itself." And God's will for today, I will add, is to love others and use our gifts to serve and honor him.

I always try to encourage doing what you love to do and what you are gifted to do. That may be your vocation or it may not be, but use your gifts for God's work. We also must throw into the recipe some common sense, a large dose of experience, and some faith. And any advice I give someone about "God's will," I do so with humility. I can't see very far into the future of my own life, much less someone else's.

I have often joked that my calling into the ministry happened right in the middle of a calculus exam. I looked up to the heavens and asked, "Is that other job still available?" Of course, that is far from the truth. I ultimately did (the ministry) what I felt called to do and what I enjoyed doing. No one twisted my arm and made me enter the ministry. God didn't hold a gun to my head and make me surrender.

For ten years or so I was a college minister. I knew that I didn't want to do that forever (too many long nights and weekends). So, I decided to give pastoring a try and found that my particular gifts fit very well in the church setting. I didn't know that when I was 18 or 28. I discovered that with some common sense, a little experience, and a measure of faith.

And I have also discovered that, as a pastor, I do get a lot of "respect." Way more than I deserve, with or without a fortune cookie.

What Letters?

When our son played baseball as a kid, we went to lots of games around this county. Sometimes the umpires were good and sometimes not. Umpires are called by a nickname—"Blue." The protective gear they wear is a dark color, sometimes blue, or maybe black. When fans want to voice their displeasure at a call, they yell something like this: "Bad call Blue," or "Blue, I've got some glasses you can borrow."

There was one umpire who had a different nickname, one that he had earned, I might add. When he umpired, strikes were called that seemed to be so far from the plate they were in Heard County. He liked calling strikes if the ball got in the same area code of the catcher. One game, and I promise this is true, a ball landed about a foot in front of home plate. He let out a hearty "Strike!!!!" The parents went ballistic!

We had a nickname for that particular umpire, though we didn't use it to his face. The nickname for him was "Cataract." When we arrived at the ballpark and saw that "Cataract" was umpiring, we knew that our kid was going to go 0 for something. Who can hit a ball that lands a foot in front of the plate?

Well, when I was a kid I went home from school one day and told Mom that I couldn't see the board. So, we went straight to see Dr. Denny, the local eye guy, and he put some letters on a wall. "Can you see the letters?" I couldn't. It didn't take long to get my first set of glasses. Dr. Denny went to the Coke machine, took out a Coke bottle and carved some out for me. Those were some more thick glasses. You put those inside some dark rims, and you will know why I had a bad year.

I graduated from Coke bottle lenses to hard contacts. And on a dusty, windy day, life was not worth living. I graduated from those to soft contacts, and I felt like I had been born again. Then several years ago, a doctor performed Lasik surgery on my eyes, and I could see like a hawk. Man, life was good.

I have spent much of my life looking at letters on a wall, and so I had a flashback recently. The good doctor asked me if I could read the letters. I pretended I was eating Alphabet cereal and started guessing. No luck. I was so afraid he was headed to the Coke machine again. Then he gave me the bad news: I have the beginnings of a cataract.

I thought you had to be 86 to have cataracts. I thought only umpires who couldn't see had them. I thought your name had to be Me Maw or Paw Paw to have them.

I don't know if Jesus had cataracts in mind when He said, "Judge not that you be not judged," but what He said sure hits home. We should be careful in calling others names lest we get the same labels when our time comes.

And by the way, if I am ever asked to be an umpire, I will say "No," and "Heck no."

There Is a Reason It Is Called Niagara "Falls"

I'm the type guy who hates roller coasters. I hold the hats and umbrellas while people like you pay hard earned money to scream your head off. Not me. I like my feet on Mother Earth. I am a great believer in what Jesus said, "Lo (w) I am with you..." (Matthew 28: 20).

I don't like heights. And I think the Wallendas are nuts. However, I have to give Nik Wallenda credit for his most recent amazing feats. He walked across Niagara Falls on a two-inch wide cable some 200 feet above the falls, with no safety net. Fighting the winds and mist, he made it in about 25 minutes. Next, he walked across the Grand Canyon, again with no safety net.

By the way, after the Niagara Falls event, as he walked over into Canada, he was met by a customs agent who demanded his passport. And when asked the purpose of his visit, Nik said, "To inspire people around the world." Well, the only thing Nik inspired me to do is not to let my kids become tight-rope walkers.

You may have heard of Nik's great-grandfather, Karl Wallenda. Besides being half nuts, they must have had a thing for k's, with Karl (Carl) and Nik (ck). Like I said, they must be a little (k)razy to do what they do. Anyway, Karl was the greatest tight-rope walker of all time. He was known for walking high in the air across great distances without a net. And it seemed that the older he got, the more amazing were his stunts. He was doing walks in his 70s better and more dramatic than what he had done in his 20s and 30s. The only walks I will be doing in my 70s will be to the mailbox and restroom.

In 1978, while performing a walk between two tall buildings in San Juan, Puerto Rico, he fell to his death. I read an interview with his wife some time after his death. She said, "It was very strange. For months prior to his last walk, he thought about nothing else. For the first time, he had nightmares about falling. She spoke of his hesitancy and how on that walk he even checked the installation and construction of the wire himself. "This was the first time," she said, "Karl had never done that."

What led to his fall? Hesitation and fear, I suppose. It's the same with me as a Christian. If I take my eyes off of my goals and put them on my problems or if I focus on my fears, then I am doomed as a Christian. I will fall too.

It is so easy to focus on the short-term fears: the latest blood work from the doctor; the latest report card from school; the evil boss at work; or a child going off to college or camp. It is hard to step back and get the bigger view, which is, that God is still there with us, and God will guide us through. I do believe that God is with us on the high-wire or low-wire, in the good times and bad, when we make it across the finish line or when we stumble and fall.

I'm just wondering if Nik spells Grand Canyon with a C or a K?

Pinetop the Piano Man

I don't know if it is something that is unique to preachers or if some of you do it too. What I do that you may or may not do is scan the AJC obituary page looking for a story. Maybe it is the preacher in me just looking for a sermon illustration, or maybe it is the writer in me looking for an idea. But regardless, I found an interesting obit.

The caption was 'Pinetop Perkins, 97.' Anyone named Pinetop would pique my interest and that was followed with the headline, 'Bluesman won Grammy this year.' The lead paragraph of the obit told me the gist of the story. Pinetop Perkins was one of the last old-school bluesmen who played with Muddy Waters; Pinetop won a Grammy this year; and Pinetop died of cardiac arrest at his home.

It told me more as I continued. He had a distinctive voice and played the piano "aggressively." B.B. King said of him, "He was one of the last great Mississippi Bluesmen...he will be missed by lovers of music all over the world." Pinetop toured with Ike Turner in the '50s and joined Muddy Waters' band in 1969. He won a Grammy in 2011 for best traditional blues album, which made him the oldest Grammy winner ever. He had an 80-year career of playing juke joints, nightclubs, and festivals.

It was a fascinating obit, but what really caught my eye was the last line: "he had no survivors." None. He apparently had no kids, no grandkids, no great-grandkids. Did he have no family at all? Think of all the stories that died when he died. He needed some family who would tell, collect, and write down all his memories of 80 years of performing in honky tonks and bars. We all need someone to pass along our stories after we are gone.

It is called the second death. Someone dies and nobody remembers them. I think deep down we all worry about that. It happens all the time, by the way—those who die alone in a nursing home or the homeless man who dies under an Atlanta bridge. Years ago I did a pauper's funeral for a lady. I was the only one at the grave. Who noted her passing? Pinetop will be remembered for his music, but who will tell his stories?

In Old Testament thought you live on after death in your kids. They become the scrapbooks that continue your life and legacy. Hopefully, they do more than tell stories about you; they also carry on your personal traits and values. You instill in them what makes you who you are and then they, in turn, do that to their kids. You teach them your faith, then they teach their kids, and on and on it goes. That way, you keep on living for several more generations.

After I am gone, my kids will tell my stories. That would mostly be stories about boring sermons and wedding screw-ups. But there will be vacations to talk about and a few jokes they will remember. Maybe, just maybe, the values that are important to me will be important to them, and they will catch on. And pass them on.

And, oh by the way, in the New Testament, not just your stories live on, but you do. By professing faith in Jesus Christ, you share in His resurrected life. Maybe in heaven Pinetop can tell us his stories; I'll bet he has some doozies.

Pain Pump

I wrote a sports' devotional book a few years ago entitled "Take a Knee." The title was based on the prayer posture that some teams take before or after a game. Well, a local orthopedic surgeon took the title literally, and he took my knee. He took out the bad one and gave me a new, though artificial one. Thus, I spent several days over the Christmas holidays in the hospital and then several recuperating at home. Cynics among us have accused me of planning my surgery around the football bowl season. Yes, the remote control may need to be surgically removed from my right hand, but given the difficulty of this recuperation, not even I would stoop to such levels.

While in the hospital I got hooked up to a pain pump, meaning that if the pain got too great, I could just hit a button, and enough pain medication would be pumped into my body to make listening to rap music soothing. As I left the hospital I went to the local pharmacist and got armed with enough pain pills to medicate the losing locker room after any number of bowl games. While, I do appreciate the caregivers' attempts to alleviate my pain, there does seem to be a tendency to run from pain in our culture. Pills and pumps can cure anything, right?

Enduring some physical pain would probably be good for us, but there are of course other pains as well. When a girlfriend during seminary days dropped me like I was some early church heretic, I could have used a pain pump or pill. That hurt like the dickens, and there was no shortcutting it. It hurt so bad I had to drag myself out of bed every day for months.

When my dad died it hurt too, and I looked around for a pain pump but found none. I understand that we may choose to medicate the pain by hugging a bottle or taking drugs. Those are not the healthiest choices, but for some they seem to be easier ones than facing that hurt head on. When my brother died unexpectedly and tragically, the pain was worse than any artificial knee. I wish I could have carried a pain pump to work, 'cause I sure needed one.

I am not some macho dude oblivious to pain. I am grateful for that pain pump and some pills to help me through some tough nights, but we have to develop some backbone and quit looking for pills and booze to make the pain magically go away. Facing our pain head on, armed with some faith and support from loved ones, is the best route to take.

Sure, we can't and shouldn't be strong all the time. Rather, we should welcome the strong shoulders of others and the "Kleenex and casseroles" that are served with love.

The Psalmist said a curious thing: "It is good for me that I have been afflicted" (119: 71). I think he meant that he had become a better, stronger person because of his suffering. And what was the nature of his suffering? I have it on good authority that he had bad knees.

The House of Pain

It's not the surgery that gets you when you have a knee replaced. It is the therapy. I ain't lying; it's pretty tough. My therapist Lew, an otherwise nice guy, turns into Lucifer. Jennifer, Lew's partner in pain, turns into Jezebel. The therapy room becomes the House of Pain. I haven't cried (yet) but I have thought about it, and I haven't cussed yet (but if someone would write the words down, I would sign it). Whoever first coined the phrase, "No pain, no gain," must have had a knee replacement.

I do appreciate both my therapists who are helping me get better each time I visit. In fact, in about a month or two I'll be dancing a Jig. Lucifer and Jezebel, oops, I mean Lew and Jennifer are really nice people who remind me of my dad, who, before whippings, said, "This hurts me more than it hurts you." "Yes, Dad, sure. It just hurts me in a different place."

I've noticed this about physical therapists. They also, from time to time, play the role of psychotherapist. I have heard folk tell the therapists about a family problem or personal struggle. Maybe it is because the therapist is yanking on your knee in such a way that you are thinking terrible thoughts and you blurt out, "Did you know I have a drinking problem?" Or as they stretch your leg into ungodly positions, you scream, "My husband is a lunatic!" without giving much thought to the consequences of such a declaration. As the pain in the knee is ramped up, perhaps patients become more open about their personal pain.

All of that reminds me of my favorite joke. A horse walks into a bar and the bartender asks, "Hey, hey, hey. Why the long face?" I don't frequent bars, but I understand that folk, after a few drinks, will open up to the bartender about life's struggles. Bartenders and therapists (OK, and preachers too) have a lot in common. People just unload on us about all their stuff. And I don't have to twist their knee or pull on their leg to hear it. (However, my sermons have been known to be painful.) Hopefully, we preachers are as good a listener as the bartender is reputed to be and as good as the physical therapist has to be.

A Christian professor wrote a book called, "How Will They Hear If We Don't Listen?" He says that instead of preaching to folk, maybe we ought to start by listening to them. Our Christian monologues, though well intended, are not very effective. Let's try some dialogue. And a good place to start is where they hurt. If you take time to listen, they will tell you. And you don't have to yank on their knee to get it. When we listen to others talk about their pain, their questions, and their doubts, then it makes us more vulnerable and approachable. It makes us better witnesses for Christ.

I have it on good authority that the Apostle James first started out as a bartender and then became a physical therapist. I know because how else would he have had the wisdom to write: "Let every person be swift to hear, and slow to speak" (James 1: 19).

Walking Dead Man

I didn't know how to take her words. Were they a "backhanded compliment"? I have heard my share of those: "You are smarter than you look;" "I didn't recognize you, you looked so good;" and "You clean up well." My all-time favorite for the preacher: "I liked last week's sermon better." Huh?

Like I said, I didn't know how to take her words. She was the lady working the concession stand at some soccer fields where our daughter was playing. She was a total stranger, so maybe she felt free to hurl some confusing words my way. What would you think if you were about my age, went to the concession stand to order a yummy hamburger, and the lady taking your order says, "I thought you were Walter Matthau." I could have come back with, "I thought you were Rosanne Barr."

It is said that Winston Churchill had the best (or worst) comeback ever when a lady said to him, "Winston, you are drunk." He replied, "Madame, you are ugly but tomorrow I shall be sober." That is a mean-spirited comeback and not one that I or any Christian should try to emulate.

I didn't say anything to the lady; I was so confused I was speechless. Was that a compliment? Walter Matthau has been dead for 12 years and so was she saying I reminded her of a walking dead man? Did she remember him from the hit movie "Grumpy Old Men," and thus I must have looked grumpy as I ordered my burger. Did she think that he was handsome? Look at his picture and decide for yourself. If she had said that I remind her of Clark Gable I would have kissed her; if she had said I remind her of Barney Fife I would have kicked her. What did she mean by the Walter Matthau comment?

Instead of backhanded compliments, how about real ones? Mark Twain once said that he could live for two months off of a compliment. Psychologist William James felt that the deepest human need is the need to feel appreciated. The writer of Proverbs says, "A tongue has the power to nourish life or kill it" (18:21).

We should all learn the habit of giving thanks to God and each other. We should find the good in others and praise it. Find the good in life and thank God for it. There was a Scottish minister who awoke one Sunday to a dark, freezing, wet, and stormy Sunday. One of his deacons whispered, "I am sure the preacher won't be able to thank God for anything on a day like this." The pastor began the service with a prayer: "We thank you Lord that the weather is not always like this."

In Old Testament days, the parent would give "the blessing" to the children, typically to the oldest child. The blessing acted on the one hand, like a will or estate plan, in which it bestowed material blessings on the child. But it also meant approval and pride. In fact, the word "blessing" in Hebrew means "to speak well of or praise." So, for the child to receive the parents' blessing meant to have their approval, to be spoken well of by the parents, and to know that the parents found delight in the child.

So, say a word of blessing to God for all you have and then to others because they are made in God's image. And be careful what you say. If you start a sentence with "You remind me of..." be oh so careful. If you finish the sentence with Walter Matthau make sure you say it to a "grumpy old man."

"Fielding" Questions From a Five-Year-Old

I don't blame him for being a tad confused. His dad is a Georgia grad and his mom is an Auburn grad. So, give the poor kid a break. His name is Field, named after a great-grandfather, Winfield. Like a lot of five-year-olds, he asks good questions. He wants to know if angels come in girl and boy models. He wants to know if heaven is in the clouds, and most of all, he wants to know where God comes from.

His mom and dad aren't trained theologians, like yours truly, but they make their best efforts at answering his tough questions. And when in doubt, they send him to the one who spent the better part of his life stuck in seminary libraries (with no social life) and who has a direct line to God himself. Are they talking about me? "Ask Preacher Steve," they tell him.

So, on a Wednesday night, the second most sacred day of the week, Field asks the religious authority in his life, the man with all the answers, the man so close to God that he and God text every day, the really tough one, "Where did God come from?"

Given his confusion about college affiliation, I didn't want to confuse him further. Thus, I decided not to go with my first answer, "Tuscaloosa." The answer I gave him wasn't very good.

After years of exile in seminaries you would think I could come up with something better. My answer was a lame, "I don't know."

I'm sure Field was disappointed in my answer, and he may not listen to anything else I ever have to say. So, why would that be any different than half my church? But maybe what I said to him is the very best thing that I could have ever said. I hope it is not the last time he hears a preacher say, "I don't know."

Unfortunately, we Christians have become known more for our cocksure attitudes than for our humility. We often act like we are the possessors of all truth on everything and our perspectives are always the correct ones. The truth is, those of us who live on biblical authority have been wrong about a lot of things. We have been on the wrong side of history on social issues (slavery) and science issues (Galileo). A large dose of humility would help our Christian witness immensely.

According to what I have read, pagan thinkers never honored humility. But read the Bible. Jesus talked freely about His most difficult moments, like when He was in the desert and tempted or when He was in the garden and His disciples fell asleep. In the Bible, Simon Peter comes off looking like a loser in Mark, a gospel that apparently depended on his testimony for material. This same Simon Peter and John, two heroes of the early church, got a little full of themselves at times, and both received strong rebukes in all four gospels.

I may not have given Field the answer he wanted, but maybe I gave him a better one.

May Fest or May Quest

All I wanted was a corn dog and a funnel cake. What I got was four gold fish. I didn't want even one gold fish. I got four. I got them at May Fest, a wonderful local, downtown festival.

I thought that we (our nine-year-old daughter and I) would come home with a couple of balloons and her face painted. I had not planned on spending a boat load of money. You know, just let her play a few games, pet a few animals, bungee jump, and eat a corn dog or two. And throw in a funnel cake for good measure. That is what I thought I would spend.

That is what I thought I would spend until she played this game straight from the county fair. You have played similar ones. You pay a couple of bucks for the privilege of tossing ping pong balls into containers. I thought if we tossed one in we would win some cheap prize. Well, we tossed and tossed. Finally we got one in; no, several in. And the lady in charge said, "Congratulations, you are a winner." "Yea, what is our lucky prize today?" "Goldfish," she said, "four goldfish."

The Davis family is not a good pet family. We have a dog, but we are not really good with her. Now we have four goldfish. I had to lug the fish around the rest of the day, dropping ice in the plastic bag so they would survive the heat. Is it wrong to pray for goldfish to die?

Goldfish can't live in our tub, so they had to have a home. They now have a $30 bowl that lights up like a disco. I'm surprised it didn't come with a Bee Gees' CD. They now have a home, with some lovely rocks to give it an aesthetic view, and ample food for the remainder of their short lives. Next year, I'm going to the bank on the way to May Fest. I'm giving the fish a week or two max, and I have already told our daughter about their life span. I told her that I don't do goldfish funerals. When they are gone, they are down the toilet.

I just preached a sermon Sunday on how God loves the whole world (John 3:16). The word world (kosmos) means not just people, but His entire created order. Kosmos means "to bring order out of chaos." We get our word cosmetics from it, by the way, so that when a woman puts on make-up, she is bringing order out of chaos. I'm guessing God's love for His created order includes lakes, rivers, flowers, and animals. And I guess goldfish are on that list. Gnats? No, and heck no, but goldfish are in.

Taking care of God's creation is actually pretty serious business. We should care about the environment and the animals of this world. We should not pollute or litter. This is God's world (kosmos).

By the way, if the ping pong ball had rung the middle container, we would have won the grand prize—a rabbit. I guess I should be grateful for small victories.

Grammatically Correct

I need one more club to join like I need a hole in the head. But I just might sign up. I'm not sure what the dues are, but perhaps I can afford it. Some causes are so just and right that the cost is worth it. I'm talking about joining the Apostrophe Protection Society of England. We have groups that work to protect wildlife and endangered species of animals, so why not apostrophes? After all, if we don't protect them now, we could lose them forever. I can't fathom life without apostrophes. Can you?

What brought this issue to the forefront was a controversy at the University of Minnesota about the name of a fancy new walkway called the Scholars Walk, as opposed to the Scholar's Walk. Larry Laukka, who heads the group developing the walkway, argued that an apostrophe would add distinction by suggesting that the walkway was owned by those it honors. But the board that had the decision making power, decided not to add the apostrophe. Said a disappointed Laukka, "I'll have to lick my wounds. But I'll get over it." (Notice that he used two apostrophes in his response.) The board ruled against the apostrophe because it would make the university appear exclusive, not inclusive. It also might have led to the adding of apostrophes to other places like Professors Lane. Said board member Margaret Colson, "Apostrophes would be out of control."

(I's all for grammatical korrectness. I are a big proponent of it. Is you two? I don't never like to make no grammatical mistakes. 'Cause when I makes them, somebodies always learning me how to do it correctly. I guess us Christians oughta care 'bout such things 'cause it makes a bad impression when we talks like a bunch of hicks. On the other hand, I's a gessin' that the good Lord cares more about the heart than he does them darn apostrophes.)

Seriously, I know the rules of grammar, but I never get them all right. For instance, I know that a preposition is not something you should end a sentence "with." Grammatical rules are good and we need some or else we would all talk like Jed Clampett or Uncle Si from Duck Dynasty. They provide guidelines for us and are ultimately for our own good. However, obsession with the rules of grammar or life will do us no good. If I lived in fear of breaking a grammatical rule, then I would never open my mouth. Conversely, obsession with God's laws will turn us into legalistic Pharisees.

It's (notice the apostrophe used correctly) more important to have your heart, than your apostrophe, in the right place. "Let the words of my mouth and meditation of my heart be acceptable in Thy sight…" (Psalm 19:14).

Beer Bath

Sheri and I celebrated 22 years together by going into Atlanta to eat at a fancy restaurant. It was a seafood place where they fly the seafood in fresh from the Chattahoochee (or wherever). Great food and service, by the way.

The highlight of the evening was not the meal but what happened at a table adjacent to us. There was a young couple drinking beer and eating something that looked crabs on steroids. He did what has happened to all of us from time to time: he knocked his drink over. If you have young kids, it happens every meal, so you like for it to happen early in the meal to get it over with. Like I said, he was drinking beer, and it went all over his clothes. His left pant leg was covered in it, as was his chair, and the suds dripped slowly off the table and saturated the floor. Being the good Baptist minister, I thought, "If he had been drinking iced tea, that wouldn't have happened." Sheri offered a napkin to help, as I tried not to laugh out loud. If I had expressed any pleasure whatsoever at his misfortune, he probably would have slugged me. And a melee might have broken out.

The German word is *schadenfreude*, which means to find pleasure in someone else's misfortune. I point out that word to impress you that I know one German word besides Volkswagen. There is a sort of malicious joy that seems to be a part of our culture. Have you noticed? Why did I find it amusing that some guy spilled beer all over himself?

Well, *schadenfreude* is in the Bible, so it has been around for a long time. When the Egyptian army is still sinking to their grave in the Red Sea, Moses and Miriam break out the tambourines and lead a mocking dance and song: "Pharaoh's chariots and his army He has cast into the sea; and the choicest of his officers are drowned in the Red Sea" (Exodus 15:4). If Miriam and Moses did it, then it's okay, right?

Schadenfreude is a national pastime. Democrats and Republicans gloat when someone from the other party is caught having an affair or embezzling money. The chuckles can be heard all the way down Pennsylvania Avenue to the Capitol and from there to Main Street USA. Remember when Martha Stewart got sent packing to prison because she apparently profited from insider trading? Lots of folk cheered her misfortune. Someone twittered on the New York Times that it was the blonde version of *schadenfreude*: *blondenfreude*—the joy of watching blondes screw up.

Gloating over someone else's misfortune is kind of sick, but it's also kind of human nature. I'm just not sure it's God's nature. And when I do it, I have an uneasy feeling that I shouldn't. Something seems amiss in my soul when I find any pleasure in another person's pain. I can't see Jesus doing it. I can't see Him gloating when a Pharisee gets arrested for breaking the law. And yet, I can find great pleasure when a Pharisaical televangelist gets caught doing something that he preaches against every Sunday.

I don't think it is right to gloat like that, but I do. I think most of us are gloaters, but should we be?

Best and Worst Day

Tornadoes forced the cancellation of the Carrollton city schools for a day. Our then five-year-old daughter went to Pre-K there and my wife teaches in that system. When we informed our daughter that school had been cancelled, she exclaimed, "This is the best day of my life!" (She loves her school and teachers, by the way.) When I reminded her that she has been to Disney and the circus, she held her position that it was the best day of her life. She's five. She has no perspective.

What was the best day of her life was the worst day for others. Some people lost their homes; thankfully, no one lost their life. A couple in our church had tree limbs the size of telephone poles through their roof and into their bedroom and hallway. There is major structural damage to their home and it will take time — lots of it — to repair the damage.

I went by their home the next day to offer what moral support I could. The look on their faces said that they were hurting — not physically — but emotionally. I have never felt as helpless as a minister. I'm not any good with a hammer. I don't know which end of a chain saw to h.... On second thought, at least I do know that. They needed things like heavy equipment to remove trees, insurance agents to assess losses, and utilities people to restore power. Thank goodness those people arrived in due time. In fact, some men from our church and a team of wonderful people from Bethany Christian Church came with heavy equipment, saws, and strong backs. Others brought food and neighbors pitched in.

I offered what I had at that time — a prayer and a hug. I wanted to offer more, but couldn't. I routinely say, when leaving a hospital or nursing home, "Call me if I can help." I stopped myself before saying it on this day. I didn't want to sound glib or insincere. They needed so much.

I am reminded of the story told about the great preacher, Dwight L. Moody. He was on a trans-Atlantic ship when the ship's boiler caught on fire. The passengers formed a water-bucket line and threw water on the fire. At a moment when it looked like the fire was out of control and all hope was gone, a young preacher tapped Moody on the shoulder and said, "We should go to the other end of the ship and pray. The only thing left now is prayer." Moody exploded and shouted to the young man, "Get in line. You can pray and pass the buckets."

At our church, we pride ourselves on the ministry of "casseroles and Kleenex." Hurting people often need both. Maybe we should add chain saws to the list.

Which Superhero Would You Be?

We found the three of us in front of the same TV. That, in and of itself, was a small miracle. Sheri and Natalie were watching a superhero cartoon when I entered the room. I caught the tail end of the program.

We then had a few moments of conversation about superheroes. I said that my favorite has always been Superman. That dude was cool. In recent years I have enjoyed the Spiderman movies and, of course, the Batman stuff as well.

Sheri, I think, asked the question, "What superhero trait would you want to have?" I immediately said that like Superman, I would want to fly. Would that be groovy or what? I could visit Atlanta hospitals, go to Braves games, etc., without any Atlanta traffic. I could fly above the traffic snarl at the I-285/I-20 junction and just wave at the hapless motorists below. I could say to Sheri and Natalie, "Hop on my back and we're headed for Panama City. We'll be there in about 30 minutes." With that ability I could rescue cats from tree tops and Frisbees from housetops.

Sheri prefers the superhero trait of invisibility. With that trait she could sneak into board rooms of corporate meetings and find out what they are up to. The invisible Sheri could go into the war rooms of other countries and get the scoop. Natalie set us straight by saying that would be wrong.

Natalie then said that telekinesis is the trait she would like. I thought that was a pretty big word coming from a just finished the third grade, nine-year-old kid. Of course, kids these days know some stuff. She said that being able to move objects with just your mind would be cool. I said, "Yes, I could get the remote without having to leave my chair." I could move ant beds from my yard to the neighbor's (nothing like loving thy neighbor, huh?), move a baseball headed for a sure out, to an over the fence home run (isn't that cheating?), or move a pile of dirty clothes from the hamper to the washer (isn't that being lazy?). Come to think of it, telekinesis might not be such a good thing.

I don't know if any of the superheroes can cure diseases, but that is a trait I would like to have. Have you ever stood next to a quadriplegic and wished for the gift of healing so that they could rise up and walk? I have. I see the blind and wish for healing so that they could see sunrises and smiles. Jesus did healings like that, but I can't. Churches do lots of things that are akin to that. We provide food for the hungry, coats for the poor, casseroles for the sick, and eye glasses for those who can't see well. It is not the same as healing but at least it is in the same ballpark. We do what we can with what we have. We all wish we could do more.

Just for one day, I would like to be Superman—"faster than a speeding bullet, more powerful than a locomotive, able to leap tall buildings in a single bound." I suppose I could do a lot of good with those powers. But come to think of it, if we were all super servants instead of superheroes, think how much we could do for the cause of Christ.

If love is the most powerful force in the world, as Paul says in Romans 8:35-39, then maybe we just need more of that. Love trumps Kryptonite any time.

Steve Davis

A Sermon in the Cereal

I can find a sermon anywhere, anytime or anyplace. I have a nose for sermons. I can find them at 7:00 in the morning when eyes are barely open and brains are just getting warmed up. I got one recently at the breakfast table—gift wrapped by our daughter.

I was shocked to hear our nine-year-old Natalie say that she doesn't like Rice Krispies. Huh? "You've got to be kidding," I said. "Every kid in America likes them. You were born in Georgia, right?" What is not to like? They taste pretty good with milk and they crackle in the bowl. Not liking Rice Krispies is like not liking apple pie. Come to think of it, she doesn't like apple pie. She has peculiar taste buds, but then again, for a nine-year-old, maybe not. She likes chicken fingers, spaghetti, mac'n cheese, and despises anything green. In spite of that peculiar list, I was shocked with the Rice Krispies rejection.

And so I gave her the speech about fruit on cereal. "Honey, just about any kind of fruit on them is delicious." She likes strawberries, and they are a natural on Rice Krispies. So, surely that would be a hit with her. Not. She informed me, "Dad, you don't mix the good with the bad."

That was my sermon; straight from the mouth of a nine-year-old. Jesus told a parable one time about wheat and weeds, or if you will, Rice Krispies and strawberries. The parable he told was about a man who planted some seeds that turned into beautiful wheat. But lots of weeds showed up in the field, and the workers came to the master and asked if they should pull the weeds. His answer: "No. Leave the weeds alone. You might pull up wheat with the weeds." In other words, let them grow side by side.

When I was in high school, Mom asked me to pull some weeds out of her flower bed. I pulled what looked like weeds and left what looked like flowers. Sometimes you can't tell the difference. Mom still hasn't forgiven me.

I know Christian people who seem to want to withdraw from the world. They don't like rubbing elbows with weeds. How sad. Jesus spent His ministry among people who didn't exactly measure up, who were on the bottom of the social ladder, or who had made a mess of life. Some might call them weeds, but Jesus didn't.

And the truth is, God can change a weed into wheat. Some folk say that people never change. I disagree. With God's grace and God's Spirit, a leopard can change its spots and the old dog can learn some new tricks. Why give up on the weeds? And why try to run from them or hide from them? They are the people Jesus died for and the people He wants us to love.

So, mix some strawberries with your cereal—the good with the bad. Not only will it taste great, but it is good theology too.

Silencing Your Cell Phones and Other Things

We got to our seats at "Madagascar 3" a little early, meaning we were there to see all the advertisements before, as well as sample all the previews of upcoming movies. Sheri, Natalie, and I went with some friends, and we settled into our seats with a big tub of popcorn shared by all. Like I said, we saw all the stuff on the screen that one sees when arriving early. If I saw it once, I saw it on the big screen a dozen times: "Psst, silence your cell phones." So, I did. I am a Baptist preacher, and I appreciate it when folk turn off their cell phones so as not to ring during the sermon.

I want to suggest that the theatre also add the words, "and your noisy kids," (and a few more words), after the "silence your cell phones." They should scroll it across the screen in big, bold print, **"Silence your cell phones and your noisy kids so that the people seated behind you can enjoy the dad gum movie that the**

three of them paid $30 to see." And they should add an exclamation point.

Seated in front of us were a young mom and her two kids. The older boy was about four or five; the younger one was going on two. Have you heard of the "terrible twos"? This kid for two hours was the embodiment of all the horror that the phrase elicits. He never sat still. He squirmed, kicked, and cried. One of his favorite things to do, and least disruptive, was turn around to our nine-year-old and say "Hi." And then "Hi" again. And again. He never stopped talking, kicking, and squirming. For two hours I watched him instead of "Madagascar 3."

The mom left the theatre with her two kids with about 10 minutes left in the movie. The cynical side of me said, "Why now? Why not stay and ruin the entire movie?" During the two hour debacle, I vacillated between cynical and Christian. The cynical side won most of the time: "She is being so rude to the rest of us." The Christian side was loving and understanding, remembering what it was like to be out in public places when one of our two started acting like a deacon's kid. Do we leave the restaurant or stay? Do I take them out in the hall and give a lecture before returning to the meeting? I have been in her shoes before, and they are not a comfortable fit.

I do think it is rude to ruin a movie for those seated next to you. I don't think fondly of rudeness, whether at the movies or on the road. She probably should have left with her kids sooner, but I also understand her dilemma. Maybe she thought her two-year-old would sit like a big kid; so she bought three tickets and paid her hard earned money for them. Having paid, she wasn't about to leave. I don't know what I would have done had I been her.

When kids misbehave during the sermon you can threaten the fires of hell and that usually will buy you some time. She apparently had no such bargaining chips. Having now had a few days to reflect, I actually feel sorry for her. This is the Christian side of me coming out, you know, compassion and stuff like that.

I hear that "Madagascar 3" is a great movie. I wouldn't know. I'll have to take your word for it.

To Tweet or Not to Tweet

I would like to think that my actions were not driven by professional jealousy. Though professional jealousy is not beneath me, and I have had my share of it, I don't think it is the culprit this time. What prompted me over the holidays to ask our son to help me set up a Twitter account was not in any way prompted by jealousy of former Pope Benedict. You probably have heard by now that the Pope does indeed have a Twitter account. He has a gazillion followers on it. I think it is cool that he is tweeting. However, I am not in the least bit jealous of that.

I asked my son for help because I do want to stay current with what is going on in this world. So, with his help, I am on Twitter under the name Wormy Davis (a high school nickname). The only problem now is that I have not tweeted one thing. If I were to tweet, what in the world would I say that anyone might be interested in? I am not going to tweet about what I am wearing today (who would care?) nor am I going to tweet what is in my buggy at the grocery store (again, who would care?).

In a similar vein, I am on Facebook, but I post comments on it about once a year. Occasionally, I get on Facebook to catch up with who else is on it, but it is not a part of my every day life.

My problem may be that I am just OD'd on words. We ministers it seems are always called on to "say a few words." I preach sermons every week, preach funerals, weddings, do a weekly Bible study, and write a column. As we say in the South, "Dems lots of words." It could be that I am not tweeting because the tweeter is just "plum tuckered out."

I was youth minister of a church in Mississippi years ago. One day the preacher of the church told me to attend this funeral that he was preaching. So, I did. I didn't know the deceased. After the funeral he told me to ride out to the cemetery with him (an odd request). I did. On the way to the cemetery, he dropped this little bomb on me. He said he had to leave and be somewhere else (t-time probably) and so he wanted me to do the graveside service. "You want me to do what?" I had been to maybe two graveside services in my life. What does one say at the graveside? Like I said, I didn't even know the deceased. Well, he was my boss, so I had no choice but to do it.

The pastor said to me "Oh, you just stand at the head of the casket and read some scripture, 'say a few words,' and have a prayer." I don't know what I read that day, but I managed to "say a few words" about someone I didn't know: "Here lies a good man."

I am pretty good at "saying a few words," with emphasis on a few. I've done funerals where two or three preachers were involved. The family asked the former pastors back and wanted them to "say a few words" at the funeral. Forty minutes later…and how many are a few? I can show up anywhere—a Sunday school party or a committee meeting—and someone will say, "Well, preacher do you want to 'say a few words'?" Ministers are good at it. The problem usually is limiting it to a few words.

If I am going to say something I would like for it to be meaningful. Recently Pope Benedict tweeted: "Without truth, without trust and love for what is truthful, there is no conscience or social responsibility…" Now those are meaningful words. Why couldn't I say something like that? OK, so maybe, I am a tad jealous after all.

Family News

Blueberry Muffin Meltdown

School has started, and I am thinking about kids. I've also got kids on my mind because of the highly publicized, recent cases of child abuse.

Children are vulnerable and easily manipulated. I manipulated our then five-year-old daughter, but I did it for her own good. It was looking like a bad morning. She was tired and grouchy, and I was trying to help her get dressed for school. At the same time, I was trying to get her to eat a muffin that Sheri had made. The muffins happened to be blueberry, which precipitated a crisis. "I hate blueberry. I thought they were chocolate," she said.

She was having a meltdown, and this morning was going downhill fast. She sobbed: "I love chocolate muffins. I don't like blueberry." I said, "Did you know that blueberry muffins can fly?" She smiled, but said, "They can't fly." I said, "Watch." I took the blueberry muffin and pretended it was a flying saucer as it hovered over the lamp and then the ceiling fan. It then made a dive towards the weepy little girl on the couch, as she smiled. "Did you know that blueberry muffins can talk?" I asked. Again, she smiled, but said they can't. It did. "Eat me," it said in a squeaky voice. "I need for the little girl on the couch to open her mouth."

Well, eventually the little girl opened her mouth to let the dive bombing blueberry muffin in. She ate the whole thing. I don't have successes like that every morning but thought that you should know when I do. Point being: I manipulated her. It was easy to do. I got her to do what I wanted her to do. I have her best interest at heart. Not everyone does.

So, yes, we need to protect them, but not over-protect them. We don't need to shelter them. We want them to be strong, not weak. We want them to be able to solve conflicts, not run from them. We want them to have courage, not fear. We need to find the balance between protecting those delicate minds and at the same time, nudging them out of the nest into the world that Christ told us to love and change.

On the way to school, Natalie would often say, "Play the Beatles CD." She knows almost all the words to "Come Together," "Get Back," "Hey Jude," and her favorite, "Help." Kids are like sponges.

At church and at home, we have the opportunity to teach our kids about the things we value. I don't expect the schools to do that. Their job is to educate. I will be responsible, along with the fine teachers at church, for the religious upbringing of my children. And if they don't get it, I have no one to blame but myself. We teach them our morals and values. They are listening to us and watching us.

I want to teach her more than words to a favorite rock song. I want to teach her how to love others, be kind, work hard, be responsible, and love God. That, my friends, can't be coerced or manipulated.

Harry or Hairy Houdini

The late comedian, George Carlin, had a great line about dogs: "What does a dog do on its day off? It can't lie around; that's its job." That is the kind of dog I wanted; that is not the kind of dog we got. The dog we got is part Terrier on caffeine. She is really hyper. Maggie also, in fairness, is a sweet and cute dog. I resented her at first because she is not what I wanted—she is what I got.

Her hyper-activity is heightened when a storm is approaching. Like lots of dogs, she seems to get really scared at any sign of bad weather. She is an outside dog during the day, so we can't always get home when a storm comes to let her in.

She has figured out recently that when a storm approaches and we aren't home, she can dig her way under our fence and out of the backyard. She must think that safety is at a neighbor's house. One day she escaped the backyard, and we could not see any sign of her escape—no digging, no holes in the fence. Thus, I dubbed her "Hairy Houdini." I scolded her for getting out to which she replied, "That was nothing," and she promptly pulled a rabbit out of a hat. (OK, I made that part up.)

She is a really good dog, but she is not what I wanted. How wide is the gap between what you wanted in life and what you got? Maybe as big as a Wal-Mart parking lot. Take heart, though Moses never shopped Wal-Mart, he once had a Wal-Mart sized dream: he would step foot in the Promised Land. That was his destiny, his dream. He deserved it, right? Consider this: "Then Moses went up...to the top of Pisgah...and the Lord showed him the whole land...and the Lord said to Moses, 'This is the land I promised to Abraham, to Isaac, and to Jacob...I have let you see it with your eyes, but you shall not cross over it'" (Deuteronomy 34: 1-4). Ouch!

That Moses moment on Mount Pisgah is one that happens all too often in real life at the foot of the mountain. The truth is, for many of God's children, the life you have is the life you have, and it is not going to change. And no amount of wishing and hoping is going to change a thing. There are some dreams that deserve a decent burial.[5]

For others, however, life has turned out better than you ever imagined; as we say, "beyond your wildest dreams." Congratulations.

But for many, not so. Sometimes real life unfolds in ways that are difficult to accept. If I could go back in time, I would make darn sure that the dog we got was a "lying around" kind of dog. The truth is, we are stuck with what we have, and we had better adjust to it. Maggie is about two-years-old, and so I had better take my

---

[5] Charles Poole, *Beyond the Broken Lights* (Macon: Smyth &Helwys, 2000) 24.

vitamins or she may outlive me. I am adjusting to life with a hyper dog; I am appreciating her good qualities and basking in how much our daughter loves her.

When Maggie was a puppy, running wildly about the house and chewing up shoes, ankles, and furniture, I had secretly hoped that she would pull a Harry Houdini and disappear (to someone else's home). I wasn't proud of those thoughts, but it was a way to reduce the gap between what I wanted and what I got. I have given that dream a decent burial, and now I am content with the cute dog we have. There, I said it.

Money Well Spent

I paid the $35 and didn't begrudge a penny of it. The $35 is what it cost for the Daddy/Daughter Dance. And though I dance like you would expect a Baptist minister to dance, and that would be poorly, dancing with my eight-year-old is wonderful. My poor dancing, by the way, is bad exponentially because of a bad knee and a herniated disc.

What is $35 when in return you get to dance with your daughter? We ministers like to quote Jesus at stewardship time when He said, "Where your treasure is, there will your heart be also" (Matthew 6:21). We then say something like, "Look at your checkbook to see what you value."

So, one night Sheri and Natalie asked me if I wanted to go shopping with them. Huh? The only reason they asked is because they were shopping for a dress for Natalie to wear to the dance. She has lots of dresses in the closet, but none were deemed worthy of the dance. They thought they would be nice and include me in the decision. Well, in a moment of weakness, I said "yes."

It should not have surprised me, but we were in the dress section of the store so long that I thought I might go nuts. Finally, Sheri and Natalie had three dresses in hand and they asked which one I liked best. (I had the feeling that I was part of a communist election.) I gave my opinion, but I quickly realized that my opinion didn't matter much. They bought the one they liked for the dance and then bought the other two just for good measure. Can you say money?

Since they settled on a black and white dress, I was told to wear my all black suit to the dance. And then I was kindly instructed to buy a solid white tie to go with it. I didn't have one, so I went to the men's section and got one. "That will look great in the picture," they said. Can you say money?

I then went by the florist to buy the wrist corsage. I got one that will, of course, "look great in the picture." The bill for that will come in the mail.

I emailed a friend who is taking his daughter too, and we arranged to meet for dinner before the dance. Does anyone give away food? And did I mention the father/daughter picture taken by the photographer at the dance?

So, let's see:
$35 for the tickets to the dance
$20 for the new dress (who knows what the other two cost)
$10 for the new tie (I got it on sale)
$15 for the corsage
$30 for dinner and
$35 for "the picture"

Dancing with a bad knee and a herniated disc: painful. Dancing with my daughter: priceless.

Black Friday

I had never in my entire life bought so much as a pair of socks on Black Friday until this year. I didn't even know why they call it Black Friday. I figured it had something to do with wearing black at funerals and men, most of whom hate shopping, said that it felt like one. I have since been corrected and now know that the black reference is to merchants getting into the black (before this recession) with their finances because of all the purchases. Like I said, I have never contributed one single dime on Black Friday, because I do hate shopping, and why would anyone in their right mind get up at the crack of dawn to do something they hate?

All of that changed one year when our son was a high school senior, and he convinced me that he would need a laptop for college. (Trust me. It does no good to tell your child that when you went off to college you got a new abacus and a slide rule. They will give you no credit for that, only a look of bewilderment.) Mind you, he was not in college yet, but he said he would need one, and what better time to get one than Christmas and what better day than that mad rush called Black Friday? I fell for it. I fell for it like the sucker parent that I am.

I have always thought that folk who get up before the rooster and rush to stores are idiots. I still think that, but feel rather hypocritical since I just did it. Most shoppers that day looked tired and grumpy (as opposed to me) and perhaps hadn't gotten their morning jolt of caffeine. "Are we having fun yet?" seemed to be the words on the lips of the Black Friday freaks that I observed.

I found some small consolation as I reached for my wallet, a wallet that had never been used that early in the morning. I was, as Tyler assured me, saving some money. Yeah right. You know that feeling don't you, when your wife spends hundreds at the mall and then comes home bragging about how much she saved? Why do I feel so sick when she tells me that? Well, before I got out of Best Buy on Black Friday, I had charged to my VISA card enough to have financed the Wall Street bail-out. (But think how much I saved!)

The older I get, the less I care about gifts for myself and the more I want to give to my kids, my wife, and to others who don't have much. I tell my family every year that socks and underwear will suffice for me, but they get me some other stuff anyway. Oh, it is nice to receive heart-felt gifts, and it really does feel good to wear new clothes, but that "good feel" doesn't last very long. I do find joy, however, in buying for others, which is what the "good book" says pleases the Lord: "for God loves a cheerful giver" (2 Corinthians 9:7).

I found out, by the way, why it is called Black Friday by asking our son to look it up on his new laptop.

Robbing Trains and Playing Cards

We all want good role models for our kids. It's a wonder that pk's (preachers' kids) don't all wind up in jail considering who they hang out with. Once, when our son was about four, we were at Applebee's with a church deacon and his wife. The deacon was all into sports, as was our son. Before you could say "extra point," they had made a paper football shaped like a triangle and were flicking it with the index finger like they were kicking field goals. The deacon would hold up his fingers to simulate a goal post as Tyler would flick it through. Sheri wasn't pleased with these proceedings in the restaurant, though I was slightly amused watching our son's enjoyment. All seemed harmless until he flicked one that would have been good from 50 yards, and it landed in the hair of a lady in the adjacent booth! You see what I mean when I say it is a wonder all preachers' kids aren't in the slammer.

Speaking of the slammer, a Baptist preacher from Missouri years ago, the Rev. Robert James, had two sons, Frank and Jesse. They were notorious train robbers and killers. Allegedly, once when Frank and Jesse were robbing a train, Jesse walked up and down the aisle with his hat held out for folk to put in their money. He approached a Baptist deacon who was prosperous looking but only put 36 cents in the hat. Jesse put his revolver against the man's head and asked if he had any more money. The deacon said he did have $18.12 in his boot but that it had been collected from the pious people in his Baptist church to be given to missionaries. Upon hearing the name Baptist, Jesse reached out his right hand and said, "Shake, brother, I'm a Baptist too." Ah, preachers' kids.

Which brings me to a recent story involving our daughter. She is now nine and has done well in life considering she has to hang out with deacons' kids all the time. She got strep throat recently and had to miss a few days of school. My wife was conveniently out of town, and so I had to scramble to stay home and get some work done too. One day I had to go into the office, and I got a deacon's wife to come over for a couple of hours to watch Natalie. When I left, Natalie had just gotten up and had fever in the night. I gave instructions about medicine to the deacon's wife and left.

I returned two hours later, expecting to find Natalie lying down with a fever. I found her fever free but on the couch playing the card game Gin with the deacon's wife. I leave her for two cotton picking hours and come home to find her playing the Devil's game! I guess it could have been worse—poker. As far as I could tell they hadn't been gambling, dancing, or doing drugs in my absence.

Seriously, I am so proud of the role models our kids have had in our church and community—and that includes deacons and their spouses. But ultimately my wife and I are responsible for the raising of our kids. If they don't turn out right, it is not the church's fault or the deacons' fault. It is also not the school's fault. That responsibility resides on our shoulders, a responsibility that we gladly bear.

My kids aren't perfect, but I don't think train robbing or the World Poker Tour is in their future.

Blue Guitar

Our then eight-year-old daughter asked Santa for a blue guitar and, by golly, she got one. She got lots of other stuff, mind you, but rest assured, she got a shiny, new blue guitar. When people ask her what she got for Christmas, her first words have been "blue guitar." "What was your favorite gift?" she is asked. "Blue guitar," she says.

Can she play the guitar? No, not yet. This is one of those Christmas gifts that has a price tag that will be paid long after December is gone. You see, we are in for some guitar lessons in the near future.

It's sort of like giving your 16-year-old a car or truck for Christmas. That price tag has lots of strings attached, strings that come in the form of car payments for years and car insurance. And did I mention gasoline? And dates to the movie? In other words, the gift of a car or truck comes with your 16-year-old's hand out reaching for your wallet.

A lot of the stuff we got for Christmas won't last past New Year's Day. Some of it won't work, and some of it will get broken. Games that kids get are played with and then forgotten before you can say "bowl game." The life size poster of Lebron James will get torn in half, and Lebron will look more like Spud Webb. Clothes will last until they tear, you spill ink on them, or you outgrow them (and given what we have eaten since Christmas, that will happen before the calendar turns). Gift cards, cakes, and fruit, though nice gifts, don't last.

At least a blue guitar is an investment in our child's future. She likes music and maybe playing an instrument will lead to good things for her. Who knows, she might be the next Taylor Swift. Then again, she might be like her old man and only play the radio or iPod.

What kind of investments are you making for the future? Oh, I don't mean stock market kind (though if you have a good tip, I will take it). I'm talking about investments in the lives of others. What things that have lasting value are you giving to those you love? Paul talks in Philippians 4:6-9 about things that should dominate our thinking and our lives. It's a pretty good list. He mentions things like truth, integrity, justice, purity, and goodness. It's just a list of basic stuff that we Christians ought to have every day and thus, ought to pass on to others every day.

You can't wrap these and put them under a tree. And you can't go shopping for them. They must be cultivated with prayer and commitment over time.

Blue guitars are easy. Paul's list is not. But Paul's list lasts longer.

Wild West

The death of actor James Arness brought back images of black and white TV and of villains lying dead on the streets of Dodge City. They were dead because Marshal Matt Dillon (played by Arness) killed them. He killed them dead. One shot did it, but only after they drew their guns first.

Matt Dillon was one baaad man. "Bad" in a good way, of course. He ruled the Wild West town of Dodge City with a calm demeanor, a quick pull of the trigger, and with a moral compass. Marshal Dillon wasn't a hero like The Lone Ranger or Superman; rather, he was more along the lines of an Andy Griffith. Matt Dillon didn't get the girl, he got shot lots of times, and he appeared vulnerable. But he was a decent, morally upright, hard nosed marshal who kept the bad elements out of that mythical, Hollywood, Wild West town.

His obituary caught my attention, or should I say, one line caught my attention. It was the line about one of his children, a daughter named Jenny, who died of a drug overdose. What struck me about it was how much different real life is from TV and movie life. In TV land, James Arness could fix most anything. If there had been illegal drugs in Dodge City, Marshal Dillon would have found a way to get rid of them. But real life, now that is another story.

By all accounts, James Arness was a good man and a good father. From what I read, he was much the same in real life as he was on the Hollywood screen. He was shy and soft spoken. A family man. A war hero. But real life is filled with some disappointments and heartaches, and there are no do-overs. You can't do a "Take two" until you get it right.

Parenting is hard work, whether you are a Hollywood actor or a minister. TV's Dodge City is myth. My home is not. I'm a good dad, but I'm not Marshal Dillon, and I can't use the force of my marshal's badge or minister's credentials to keep all the bad stuff away from my kids.

When you read the Bible, you see how troubled most families were in those days. Adam and Eve had two boys; one spent life on death row for killing his brother. King David's family? Solomon's? Can you say dysfunctional?

So, it seems that whether your family is living in the Garden of Eden, in a King's palace, in Hollywood or Carrollton, GA, it is never easy. But it's fun, and I wouldn't trade it for a star on the Hollywood Walk of Fame.

Daddy/Daughter Bonding

I have had lots of great bonding with our son over the years. He played sports, and I love sports, and so we bonded on the baseball field, basketball court, and golf course. We talked sports; we played sports. We bonded.

Bonding with an 8-year-old daughter is different. She does play sports, and so we do some of that together. She also does other stuff with which I am not familiar. She shops. I have heard of shopping. Someone told me that females do it with frequency and have been doing it since the beginning of time. I have also heard of places called malls, but I also heard that men weren't allowed in such places. Well, I was wrong, of course. Recently I entered one with Natalie, with fear and trembling, I might add.

Before you could say "pre-teen" we were buying shoes. These are shoes that look like old Converse low-tops, except that these are a funky color, and they have no shoe strings. They have holes for shoe strings, but you can't fit shoe strings in the holes. Go figure. It's the cool look these days. Cost me 30 bucks, and she got no shoe laces.

Next stop: bookstore. I had hoped to leave there without reaching for the wallet. Think again. I forked over some bucks for an art/reading book. I figured that was a good investment.

As we were leaving the mall (none too quickly for me), a man running one of those booths in the hallway called to Natalie and asked if she wanted her hair curled. He was selling curling irons. Natalie has straight hair, and the notion of having some curls enticed her. So, she sat, while some man I have never met starts curling her hair. I never had that experience with our son.

I'll admit that her hair looked good! But then the dude tried to sell me a curling iron for my kid. All he wanted was 90 bucks! I said "no" and "heck no."

Saying no is part of being a good parent. We live in a culture where saying yes is valued. We say yes when we get married. We say yes when asked to serve on a church committee. We say yes to community service. Saying yes is cool because it means we are valued and someone wants or needs us.

Saying no is not as valued. But saying no is as important as saying yes. We can't let our kids have everything they want. We can't say yes to every fad. "No, you can't have a cell phone...yet." "No, we aren't going to spend $90 on a curling iron." Saying no may be the very best thing you can do as a parent.

And by the way, I still prefer sports bonding to shopping bonding. And it's not even close.

Birthday Present

I knew exactly what she meant when she said it. We've been married 22 years, and with those years I have learned to read body language, interpret catty remarks, and even translate female hieroglyphics when needed. So, when she said of her approaching birthday, "I have *enough* (emphasis mine) jewelry," I knew what she meant. You see, in recent years my quest for the perfect birthday present, Christmas gift, etc. has landed me in the jewelry section. I didn't realize, until her comment, that she was ready for a gift that didn't dangle from her neck or wrist, or attach itself to her fingers. I took the hint.

Well, not only did she tell me what she didn't want, she told me what she wanted. Hallelujah, what an easy shopping trip this will be. My wife is not one to get overly sentimental. She prefers a plant instead of flowers on Mother's Day. She likes things that are useful and practical. Once I got her a new lamp pole for our walkway on her birthday, and you would have thought I was Brad Pitt.

What did she want this year? A fire pit. (And no, this was not a veiled reference to our romantic life.) You see, our daughter is having some girls over for her birthday in a week or two, and we are going to roast marshmallows and make S'mores. We need a fire pit. So, a quick trip to Target, and I was done with her birthday shopping. Our daughter wrapped it; I will put a bow on it and buy a card. They only come in one color. If she doesn't like it, what is she going to say? "I wanted a fire pit in pink."

It's now the time of year to start shopping for those we love for Christmas. In fact, Black Friday is the busiest shopping day of the year. Not for me, by the way. One could get hurt shopping today. But, regardless of when we shop, we all seek the perfect gift for that special someone. I don't know if a fire pit qualifies.

The perfect gift has two qualities. One, it certainly would be something that the special someone wants and needs. If I give my wife a dozen golf balls for Christmas, how would that qualify as perfect? Now, a dozen plants for the yard might fit the bill. Two, the perfect gift also must reflect something of the nature of the giver. If I give her something that is so out of character for me, then it doesn't qualify as a perfect gift.

We Christians like to speak of Jesus Christ as God's gift to the world. That gift meets the wants and needs that we have: love, forgiveness, and grace. And that gift is reflective of who God is—

a compassionate, loving God. As you make tracks in the malls this Christmas, take time to reflect on the greatest gift of all—God's only son.

Meanwhile, when I shop for Sheri this Christmas, I know I can't get jewelry or a fire pit. What's left?

"I Have a Dream"

My mom gave me speeches just as your mom did you. The one I remember best is the one about cleaning my plate because there are hungry kids in China. I never quite got the connection between eating my green beans and helping a hungry kid half-way around the world. I was willing to make a sacrifice to help someone else, but I thought that eating green beans was a steep price to pay. But I got the message: There are hungry kids in the world, and you are not one of them.

I have given my kids speeches too. I recently gave our eight-year-old daughter one on the way to school. It wasn't just any school day; it was the first day of school. And it was a speech she has heard before. The speech goes something like this: "Have a great year. Be a good leader in class. Learn a lot and have fun. Make new friends and care especially for the kids who look scared or who need a friend." She and her brother have heard that one before.

As I neared the finish of the well-worn text, she interrupted me and asked: "Is this the 'I Have a Dream' speech?" And then she added, "Are you Martin Luther King?" Well, yes and no. The "no" answer first. No, I am not MLK, and I could not say and speak with the words and passion that he did. Oh, how I wish I could. Now to the "yes" answer. Yes, it was my "I Have a Dream" speech. It was delivered to an audience of one, not thousands.

I have a dream for my kids just like you do for yours. And if I don't deliver that speech, then how will they know what it is? Lots of parents have dreams for their children, but they never tell them.

The speech you give your kids should reflect your values. If making all A's is the most important thing to you, then that will be reflected in your speech. If being kind to others and caring about the neglected are important to you, then that will be reflected in your speech. If standing up for yourself is tantamount, then you will say it and if "turning the other cheek" is, then you will say it.

When we have had parent/teacher conferences over the years, we have made it a point to ask the teachers how our kids are treating others in the class, especially those from other races, and if our kids are respecting the teacher. I don't care if they make all A's and are Valedictorian. If they aren't doing those other things, then they aren't doing what we want them to do, and more importantly, what Jesus wants them to do.

Someday I would like to take Natalie to the Lincoln Memorial to show her where the original "I Have a Dream" speech was delivered. But until then, from the front seat to the back seat will have to do.

"Hey, Jack, Who Stole My TV?"

When I get home at night after a long day, sometimes I want to plop down on the couch and act like a lazy bum. My wife says "sometimes?" I do like to watch TV, but mostly it is sports— Braves, Hawks, or some college b-ball. I don't have a regular network show that I watch. I don't, but I can't say that for my family.

At those times when I want to be the lazy bum preacher (I know, I know, we only work one day a week), I come home and the family has stolen my TV. When I say my TV, I mean the nice one in the living room that has high definition, not the small one in the bedroom. When I say stolen, I mean they have it, I don't, and if I want to watch something on it I have to watch what they are watching. It has gotten to the point where, before my key is in the front door, I can tell you what they are watching: "Duck Dynasty."

Sheri and Natalie are hooked on it like the first time I tasted boiled peanuts. So, my choices are to watch it or watch college basketball on a TV the size of a basketball in LD (low definition). So, I sit and watch. To the uninitiated, "Duck Dynasty" is a show on A&E about a family in Louisiana, the Robertsons, who are by their own admission, rednecks. They just happen to have made millions with a duck call business that is family run. The family is full of Louisiana characters (chief of whom is Uncle Si, "Hey, Jack...") who seem to be more about mischief than about work.

This is, so called, "Reality TV." However, it is very much staged for the cameras. But, I have to admit, it is funny as heck, with some good life lessons thrown in. I do enjoy watching it from time to time though I am not hooked like some others I know.

One recent episode had a grandchild, age 13, on her first date with her boyfriend. Her dad, Willie, the CEO of the company, is scared out of his mind about his little baby girl on her first date. He decides to take the boy, Beau, hunting to find out more about him and, in that culture, hunting is a way to prove his worth. The dad drills the poor boy with every question you can imagine, and since Beau proves himself good with a rifle (he shoots a snake), he passes the "daddy test" and is deemed fit to date his daughter.

I told Natalie I am going to take her first date to the golf course to prove himself to me. If he can grip a club and swing it OK, then he has a chance to date my daughter. If not, too bad. I'm like Willie; I don't think there is a guy in this world good enough to date Natalie. If he passes a police background check, comes from a good family, is studying for the ministry, and has a 4.0 GPA, then maybe he gets a pass. I know that I will say to him what Willie said to Beau: "You make her cry, I will make you cry."

Is there any greater love in all this world (and the other world of Louisiana) than a parent for their kid? The Bible tells us that God loves the whole wide world like a dad does his daughter or a mom loves a son. How can that be? I have known it from the first day our son and daughter were born, but it got reinforced by a long-bearded red neck from Louisiana.

Building a Gingerbread House

Parents were invited to the school to help their five-year-olds build a gingerbread house and to celebrate a holiday breakfast. So, I went. I had never built a gingerbread house; in fact, I have never built anything of substance. I'm the kind of guy who gets lost in Home Depot. The nice teacher told us parents and the kids how to use the milk carton, graham crackers, peppermint sticks, M&M's, etc., to build one and then asked us to help the kids who didn't have a parent there. I was impressed with how many parents were there, knowing that others couldn't get off work.

My daughter kindly told me that she didn't need any help, which freed me up to help a little boy seated next to her. I don't know if his dad had to work and couldn't be there or if his dad is even involved in his life. But he was a cute little guy and we set out to build a gingerbread house. I let him have all the ideas about how he wanted it to look. He was so proud of the finished product, though truth be known, it looked like Dorothy's house after the tornado in Kansas hit it.

We only had about thirty minutes of this male bonding/building thing going on. But I wish he and I had more time together besides just building a gingerbread house. You can't build a house in thirty minutes and you sure can't build a home. I wondered what his home life is like and if his dad helps him build things, or plays ball with him or reads to him at night? You can't build a home in thirty minutes and you sure can't build a relationship in that time. I wondered about his relationships. Is there someone to believe in him and encourage him?

I believe that everyone is made in God's image (Gen. 1:27). And this little guy who sits next to my daughter everyday at school is just as important to God as she is. She is lucky. She has two parents who love her and encourage her everyday. She has two parents who say to her everyday, "I love you." We sing the song at church, but do we really believe it?

> Jesus loves the little children, all the children of the world.
> Red, yellow, black and white, they are precious in His sight,
> Jesus loves the little children of the world.

You couldn't make a better Christian resolution than to become a mentor for some kid, or volunteer time at a children's home or at your kid's school.

Generation Gap (Buick Blues)

We spent spring break in Memphis where our son, Tyler, was in a baseball tournament. I have tried over the years to interest him in Elvis stuff, but to no avail. I practically begged him to visit Graceland while in Memphis, but he made it quite clear that he doesn't care much for Elvis. I should be content with the knowledge that he does like The Beatles, James Taylor and "The Andy Griffith Show" reruns. I must be doing something right.

They call it a generation gap. Parents like one style of clothes, music and vehicles, while their children prefer another. I look back on the '60s when I grew up and the clothes were, quite frankly, awful. If you look up the word "ugly" in the dictionary, you'll see clothes from the '60s. The music of the '60s—now that is different. I loved that music and our son does too, with the notable exception of the King of Rock 'n' Roll. As a parent of a teenager, I am trying really hard to listen to and like the music (I do like Maroon Five and The Fray), fashions and automobiles of his generation.

Speaking of automobiles, a few years ago I drove a Buick Lesabre, a car that our son despised. None of his friends' parents drove that make and model and he called it the "preacher mobile," which interpreted meant, "not cool." He hated that car and was embarrassed to be seen in it. When I took him to school, he wanted to be dropped off in Heard County. He said he would walk the rest of the way. Well, his prayers were answered one day when a young college girl decided to play bumper cars with my beloved Lesabre and made it look like a pretzel. The young lady who hit me was OK, and I kept assuring her at the accident scene not to worry about it. In fact, I told her that my son might want her autograph. She had done what he had only dreamed of doing. The word "totaled" brought a smile to his face as wide as a SUV.

Jesus came into this world at a certain time and into a particular culture. He may not have particularly liked their customs (we don't know for sure), but He adapted to them. As Christians, we are not to love this world (1 John 2:15), but we are to be a light to it (Matthew 5:14).

I am determined not to talk to our children about the "good ole days." They weren't as good as we imagine. As Will Rogers said, "The good ole days ain't what they used to be and probably never were." If we want to reach our culture and our children, we had better not automatically condemn it or them. If we do, then the "gap" will become a chasm.

Sportsaholic

Our daughter has seen probably 500-600 ballgames in her eight years of life. Most of them were not her choice. Our son played sports—basketball and baseball, and so when she was born, she went, crib and all. For the first six years of her life, she went with us to all his games, that is, until he went to college. She has since played some sports—soccer, softball, basketball, etc. Her latest thing is that she wants to go fishing. She says that since she is "double jointed" she should be good at it, "since you have to reel them in real fast." I know that makes no sense, but she is a girl and at this point, much of what she says fits in that category.

We have told her a thousand times that if she doesn't like sports, then that's OK. We want her to like what she likes and do what she wants to do, whether that is sports, art, or music. We have never pushed her to do anything, always following her lead. She has enjoyed the sports that she has played but not to the degree that our son did.

My wife says that our home is a shrine to ESPN. It is true that Sportscenter is on our TV more than news or soaps. It is also true that we tune in to lots of Braves' games and college football games. And if Norway is playing Sweden in soccer or tiddlywinks, we probably have it on. So, Natalie not only has gone to hundreds of games, but she has been exposed to countless others, by virtue of being my kid.

I noticed about a month ago when we attended a Braves game as a family, that she asked lots of good questions about the game. Then a couple of days later, she sat on the couch with Tyler and watched

Sportscenter highlights. I thought, "Something is going on here." Well an epiphany occurred the next day. I was at a gym exercising (that was not the epiphany) when I got a text from Sheri. The text said, "Your daughter is sitting by herself on the couch watching Sportscenter." I was as proud as when she took her first step. I showed the text to several guys at the gym as if she had just won Olympic gold.

The truth is, it would really be cool if she does like sports, but if she likes music, art, or parachuting, well, that is fine too (except for the parachuting). And I tell her that all the time. But kids do pick up on what they see and hear. Good or bad, they are like sponges and absorb so much more than we think. And the things we value, often become things they value. I hope she doesn't think that sports are a god to be worshipped, but she could, having grown up in my house.

When Natalie grows up, I hope Sheri sends me a text at the nursing home: "Honey, you would be so proud. Natalie is sitting on the pew at church worshipping without any prompting from me." That's much better than sitting on the couch watching Sportscenter. And I hope that at church, she is not a spectator.

"And you shall love the Lord your God with all heart and with your soul and with all your might. And these words, which I am commanding you today, shall be on your heart; and you shall teach them diligently to your sons (and daughters) and shall talk of them when you sit in your house (while watching Sportscenter)..." (Deuteronomy 6:5-7).

How to Pick Up a Woman

After a recent mission trip to East Tennessee, Natalie and I stopped at Dollywood for some fun. Notice I said "some," not a lot. She loves those type places, while I do not. She loves roller coasters, while I would rather ride on the hood of Earnhardt Jr.'s car than get on one of those.

There is a section at Dollywood that is like any county fair, complete with Ferris wheel, cotton candy, and lots of games where you can attempt to win stuffed animals by throwing away your money. If I had a nickel for every time I shot a basketball trying to win a teddy bear for a girl, I would be a rich man. Well, did you ever try to throw the rings onto bottles? It is pretty much impossible to do—sort of like throwing a hula hoop over a building.

It cost $5 for a bucket of rings; I gave in and let her try one bucket. The lady working the game said that the previous day no one had won. Hundreds of people had tossed thousands of rings without any success. On about her fourth attempt, Natalie flung one like a Frisbee; it hit the side of a bottle, shot in the air and came down on one for a winner. How could we be so lucky (or unlucky)? Well, they don't give out small prizes. Oh no. We won a red ladybug that is about five feet wide and five feet tall.

It weighed more than Natalie, so I had to decide whether to carry the ladybug over my shoulder or carry Natalie. As we walked around the park, every one over the age of 10 pointed at me and laughed. I offered to sell it, but no one in East Tennessee is that stupid.

As we slowly walked across the parking lot to the car, with the ladybug in tow, I asked Natalie what we should name it. I said, "It was a million to one." She immediately responded, "Mildred— Million to One Mildred Davis." So, now Mildred sits on the floor of our den like a new, rather large, piece of furniture. Natalie will probably take Mildred off to college in about nine years, and then I can have our den back.

So, that my friends, is how to pick up a woman. Sorry to disappoint. The title was more exciting than the article, which reminds me of the sermon title on the display board outside a church: "Under the bed sheet." The church was packed that Sunday only to be disappointed to find out that the preacher had covered the communion elements with a bed sheet.

Just as an article for a newspaper should live up to its title, so too our lives should live up to our title: Christian. Paul says we Christians should "walk in a manner worthy of the Lord" (Colossians 1:10). That seems really hard to do. "Walking worthy of the Lord" is a pretty tough challenge—a lot tougher than writing a weekly column for the paper.

By the way, if you really do want to pick up a woman, Mildred is available—for a price.

The PCB Olympics

If I were you I would go ahead and book your vacation for four years from now. Book it for the weeks of the Olympics. We went to Panama City Beach, with about a half million of our closest friends, recently for vacation, and it just happened to be during the Olympics. So, when we were not hanging out at the pool, building sand castles, watching movies, or playing golf, we watched the Olympic Games from London.

We were treated to some wonderful athletic achievements and some great, heart-warming stories, as well as some cruel losses and failures. The cruelest loss, however, came not from London but from Putt-Putt at Panama City Beach. I am recommending, by the way, to the IOC that Putt-Putt be added to the list of events. You see, the Davis family vacation always includes a very competitive round of Putt-Putt/Goofy Golf among the four of us. All we need for it to feel like the Olympics is a few judges or referees.

Like I said, it is highly competitive. My wife doesn't play golf anymore. She did 20 years ago, but she only touches a golf club now once a year, and it happens to be one of those cheap Putt-Putt putters, built more for swatting flies than putting a golf ball. I, on the other hand, play golf, and very well, I might add. Our son also plays golf and well. So, there is no way on God's green earth that this match should be competitive between me and Sheri. You have competition only when the score is close.

Well, she can putt. I don't know how she can 'cause she doesn't practice. Let me tell you, she can really putt. And on top of that, she is the luckiest person on the face of the earth. When I win these matches, it is skill, and when she wins it is luck. What else do you call it when someone putts a golf ball up a ramp, through a wind mill, off a brick or two, and into the hole?

Well, she won. And I am none too thrilled about it. (Lest you think I'm exaggerating, she also won two years ago and the year before that.) Actually, this year I finished third out of four. I beat our nine-year-old daughter. I won the bronze medal; Sheri won gold. I will hear about it for a year until I have a chance at redemption. This has got to stop.

I know that competition has its place. It can be healthy. It can push us to do our best; it can teach us not to accept mediocrity. Our economic system is built on it—you must outdo the next guy. But I also know that unbridled competition leads to conflict. And I know that our worth shouldn't be measured against the performance of others (though I felt like a louse for 24 hours after my humiliating defeat).

The Apostle Paul, who apparently never lost to his wife in Putt-Putt, once wrote, "Do nothing from selfish ambition or conceit, but in humility regard others as better than yourselves" (Philippians 2:3).

In the meantime, does anyone know some place close by where I can practice putting through a clown's nose?

"Well, I Made It"

The only time in your life when you like to get old is when you are a kid. Ask a child how old she is and she will say "four and a half." And kids can't wait to get to the next birthday. They can't wait to be five. You are never thirty five and a half. Never.

I love George Carlin's routine (I paraphrase it) on aging, where he says that when you become a teenager you jump to the next year. "How old are you?" "I'm gonna be sixteen." And the greatest day of your life is when you become 21. The words sound like a celebration. You BECOME 21. But then you turn 30. It sounds like soured milk. Oooh, he turned, we had to throw him out. You BECOME 21, you TURN 30 and then you're PUSHING 40. Whoa! Put on the brakes. It's all slipping away and before you know it, you REACH 50. And all your dreams are gone. But wait, you MAKE it to 60. You didn't think you would.

So you BECOME 21, TURN 30, PUSH 40, REACH 50, and MAKE it to 60. You have built up so much speed that you HIT 70. When you get into your 80's every day is a complete cycle. You HIT lunch, you TURN 4:30 and you REACH bedtime. And it doesn't stop in the 90's. In the 90's you start going backwards. "I was just 92." And then if you ever make it to 100, you become a little kid again. "I'm a 100 and a half."

When you make it to 60, which I did last week, you get all kinds of cards, such as, "What's the best thing about being 60?" You open it up and on the inside is nothing. The elderly comedian George Burns was once asked, "What's the best thing about being in your nineties?" He said, "The lack of peer pressure."

Well, the church threw a nice party for me on my 60th. They tried to make me feel better with cake and punch. The biggest punch was thrown the very next day. Mother Nature played a cruel joke on me. As if to remind me that the party was over and growing old is not for sissies, I got a kidney stone. I'm talking the very next day. When I made it to 60, plus 24 hours, I got the baddest dude in town. I wasn't sure what or who would pass first, me or the kidney stone. As I was planning my funeral, it passed, and I put those plans on hold.

As the kidney stone hit me like a two ton truck, I quoted scripture. I never knew till last week that King David had a kidney stone. But after reading the 23rd Psalm, "Yea, though I walk through the valley of the shadow of death," I am convinced of it. Or you might think I would go to a passage such as Matthew 11: 28, "Come to Me, all who are weary and heavy laden, and I will give you rest." Weary and heavy laden aren't strong enough words.

No, I went to Ecclesiastes 12 where the writer says: "Remember thy creator in the days of thy youth, before the evil days come and the years draw near when you will say, 'I have no delight in them.'" Is he saying that the 60's are evil days and I can search for delight but not find it?

I'm just hoping that the rest of my days in the 60's are better than my first day.

Having Kidney Stones and Having Babies

Many years ago the mothers of America got together and hatched the idea that men should be in the delivery room. Though I was not invited to that meeting, I assume the rationale for such a decision was that men are wimps. So, the wives thought that by getting the men into the delivery room to witness the birth of their child it would prove how tough women are and how not so tough men are. The women said, "Men think they are tough because they played football in high school and sit in deer stands in sub-freezing weather and shoot Bambi. We'll show them who's tough."

There may have also been some fluffy, spiritual rational for having us in the delivery room—men should get to witness first hand the miracle of birth. I have my doubts if the fluffy, spiritual reason really had any bearing on it at all. I figure the women just felt like it was time to show us how hard it is to have babies and in the process to laugh at us as we pass out at the sight of blood.

When my three brothers and I were born my Dad paced the floor of the hospital waiting room, smoking a cigarette, and waiting on the good doctor to bring the news. The doctor said with each one of us: "Congratulations, Mr. Davis, it's a boy—ten fingers; ten toes; baby and Mrs. Davis are fine." Dad breathed a sigh of relief, but he never passed out.

I have been in the delivery room for the birth of both of our kids, and though I didn't pass out, I thought about it, and I got as queasy as a man can get. Though there is something wonderful about being in the room for the birth of your child, it is also the same room in which you ask your wife, "What can I do to help?" and she tells you to "shut up and sit in the corner." How spiritual is that? I'm glad that my wife and I are through having kids, because I would have the tough decision of being in the delivery room again or pacing the floor (minus the cigarette) like my Dad did. I've had about all the delivery room experiences that I want in a lifetime.

Which brings me to kidney stones. I have heard it said, even by women, that having a kidney stone is harder than having a baby. I had a kidney stone two or three weeks ago, and I'm thinking maybe they are right.

In recent years I have had a herniated disc, therapy from knee replacement, and now a kidney stone. I know a thing or two about pain. Now, when church members tell me that they have pain, I listen more intently, I feel their pain more deeply, and I am better able to minister to them. Before all this happened to me, I had no idea how much people really do hurt and how pain can affect us. Now, when I read Isaiah 53:4, I understand at a deeper level what it means to say that God knows our pain, "Surely our griefs He himself bore, and our sorrows He carried." By the way, I don't think a kidney stone can hold a candle to a cross.

My wife has had two kids. I've had one kidney stone. I'm calling it even.

Halloween Revisited

Most recent Halloweens have seen me behave as an adult. But there is something left over from childhood that is hankering to come out. I decided that this Halloween would be different. I wanted to bring a little spark to our festive fall seasonal celebration. Halloween at the Davis household had become a bit boring in recent years. So, I plotted to scare the living daylights out of the neighborhood kids this Halloween. For some sinister reason (that only intensive psychotherapy could explain), I set out to make every kid in the neighborhood scream "bloody murder."

And how would I accomplish this, short of a life size cut-out of Hannibal Lecter or Darth Vader in the front yard? I thought about dressing up as a preacher and coming to the front door preaching a sermon. That has spooked many a church member over the years and has led them to soul searching and prayer. I also considered purchasing a Charlie Sheen mask, but I was afraid a party might break out. Hiding in the bushes and lurching at kids as they came up the sidewalk was also considered. That idea was scratched when I realized that I might have the energy for maybe one lurch.

What I decided to do, with Natalie's help, was to purchase a plastic spider that you hang above your front door. When someone comes to the door (poor, unsuspecting kid) and makes a motion beneath the spider, it comes down its web and lands right in front of the victim's face. (Yes, you can buy fright at the store.) The spider is big, black, and creepy and would scare the bajeebies out of Chuck Norris. This spider would turn Stephen King into a writer of children's bedtime stories. So, we bought the spider and anticipated with glee little kids screaming "bloody murder" on our front porch. What fun!

Well, after the purchase I dropped Natalie off at home, and I ran some errands. And that is when my sinister wife and daughter went to work. You guessed it. They hung the spider above the door, eagerly anticipating my return. They got their wish. As I fumbled to get my key in the door, our hairy, scary friend dropped right in front of my unsuspecting face. I'm just hoping that no one was in the bushes filming the sequel to the movie "Arachnophobia." I screamed "bloody murder," while Sheri and Natalie laughed their heads off.

Life has a way of giving us rather large doses of our own medicine. What we try to do to others often finds its way home. The old phrase works here, "What goes around comes around." I don't know if Jesus knew that phrase, but He said much the same thing: "Do unto others as you would have them do unto you" (Matthew 7:12).

The writer of Ecclesiastes must have tried a prank or two on others in his day: "Whoever digs a pit will fall into it" (10:8). Well, I dug it and fell into it, much to the delight of my wife and daughter.

Peter Panned Out

I could tell by the silence on the other end of the phone that I had said the wrong thing. When Sheri spoke, her tone of voice only confirmed that I had indeed messed up. What I said can wait until a later paragraph. It's what led to it that matters.

It all started with word that the showing of "Peter Pan" at the Carrollton Cultural Arts Center was terrific. We knew some of the people in it, including a teaching colleague of Sheri's, as Captain Hook. In addition, a kid from our daughter's class was in it, as well as one from church, and some that my wife had taught. Needless to say, we needed and wanted to go see it. So, I got three tickets, and we planned to make the Friday night program.

Here's where it gets tricky. You see, I wasn't raised going to plays and musicals. I was raised going to ballgames and golf courses. I am exposed to cultural events from time to time, and I am the better for it. I know that, and so I usually don't complain too much when going to see a play, a musical, or opera. I know that at some level, I need that.

I was excited about the "Peter Pan" thing as well, looking forward to an evening with wife and daughter. That's when my phone rang on Friday afternoon, and the caller was the Devil himself. OK, it was really our Minister of Students. He informed me that he and his wife were going to a local restaurant that night to watch the NCAA March Madness. It just so happened that they were going to watch Baylor (my sentimental choice in the tourney), and they wanted to know if I could join them.

Temptation comes in many forms. Some are tempted to abuse alcohol or drugs, others are tempted with pornography, or to steal from their company or cheat the government. Not me. I am tempted sometimes to settle for what is good when I could choose the best. I am tempted to fall back to what is familiar and comfortable instead of doing what is new or daring. My temptation often is to choose what I really want to do instead of what is best for others. And so our student minister was wearing a red cape and carrying a pitch fork when he called me. Temptation jumped out of that phone and grabbed me around my sports-crazed neck. Basketball game or musical? Self or family?

That's when I called my wife and said the wrong thing. Immediately, I knew I had. Unless you just got back from your honeymoon, then you have at some point in your marriage, said the wrong thing and knew it. I could tell by her silence at first and then her tone of voice, that I had really pulled a bad one. You see, I asked her what she thought about her and Natalie inviting a friend to use my ticket, and I would watch the ballgame. Bad move.

Years of marriage have taught me how to recover from a turnover (oops, a basketball term). I quickly apologized. And yes, I went to see "Peter Pan," which was, by the way, an amazing performance. I could have gone to watch a basketball game, but I would have missed the smiles on my daughter's face, and a smile, not a frown, on my wife's as well.

Temptations are very real. Sometimes they look like Captain Hook. Sometimes not.

Reading the Fine Print

A few days ago, the nice girl behind the Chick-fil-A counter told Natalie, "I sure do like your hair wrap." I then said to Natalie, "Tell the nice girl how much it cost." Natalie rolled her eyes, having heard or told the story on several occasions. That story has been told over and over because I think it is funny, though at the time, I found no humor in it.

It happened at Panama City Beach this summer on vacation. We were at Pier Park, a popular hang out, with shops, restaurants, movies, etc. Sheri and Tyler were at Target, while Natalie and I were on our own. We walked past a sidewalk booth that did hair stuff for girls. When I say stuff, I don't really know what to call it, except stuff—you know, hair wraps, feathers, and the like.

Natalie tugged on my shirt to get my attention, pointed to a sign at the hair booth and said, "Dad, it only cost $2.90." At this point in the story, her memory differs from mine. I think she said for that price she could get a hair feather. Have you seen these feathers? Lots of little girls have them, and they are really cute. I'm a sucker for anything cute for my kid. I did see the sign that read $2.90, but I thought it was for the feather. So, I thought, no big deal, good price. "OK, you can get one." Experience should have taught me to ask more questions, but on vacation my brain doesn't work. Tony Bennett left his heart in San Francisco, and I left my brain in Carrollton.

So, as she sat down to get what I thought was a $2.90 hair feather, I turned my attention to people watching. After some time, I decided to turn around to see how things were going, not knowing how long such a procedure takes. Much to my surprise, she wasn't getting a feather, but rather she was getting a hair wrap. That is when I read the fine print under the advertisement for hair wrap. The fine print almost gave me a myocardial infarction, otherwise known as a heart attack. It said, "$2.90 per inch." One quick glance and I knew this hair wrap was about the size of a foot long hot dog.

I paid $42 for a hair wrap! Since this article goes out to Christian audiences, I can't tell you what Sheri said.

The lady at the hair rip-off place, I mean booth, did say the hair wrap would last at least four months. I said it had better last six, and "Merry Christmas Natalie." I will put a bow on it in December.

Back to the nice girl behind the Chick-fil-A counter; after hearing a condensed version of the story, she smiled and said, "That will teach you to read the fine print." I think that the hair rip-off place should have had a sign in big, bold print: **We cater to girls, and we are out to get your money.**

When we left the hospital with a girl nine and a half years ago, the hospital should have given me some instructions in bold print: **Warning: Girls don't operate like boys.** With our son, we never had to deal with hair wraps or feathers, melt downs in the morning over what to wear, or hurt feelings over not getting a birthday invitation. No one warned me about such things.

I know the Apostle Paul said, "Love is patient," but perhaps he meant to say "Love overlooks the fine print." Maybe Paul had a son, but I'll bet you anything he didn't have a daughter.

Nicknames

If you didn't have a nickname you were nothin'. That's the way it was with my growin' up golfin' buddies. Everybody had one: Sly, Vick, Duck, Head, Shug, and Bulldog. Mine was Wormy, which, by the way, was the worst one. What chick in her right mind wanted to date a guy called Wormy? So, I tended to date girls who weren't in their right mind.

Steve Davis

The thing about nicknames is you don't get to pick your own. Somebody else picks it for you. In my case, since I resembled a worm with my body build, I got stuck with it. I would have preferred a nickname such as Pencil, or Stick, or maybe even Q-tip, but like I said, you don't get to pick your own nickname.

By the way, we are at the beach this week on vacation. As a kid nicknamed "Wormy" the beach was the last place I wanted to be. I had to have suspenders to hold up my bathing suit. Made for some bad tan lines.

Several of my classmates got together a couple of years ago at a high school class reunion, or as some would call it, a gathering of "fat fullbacks and aging homecoming queens." It was our 40th. We had a couple of parties and a memorial service. It was a really big graduating class, and some 25 of our classmates have died. I spoke at the service and reflected on how your perspective changes when you are 58, as opposed to 18. We had a good class, and most of my classmates have done well. Have we changed the world? Not hardly, but we have made, I am sure, some difference in it.

Jesus had a motley crew of twelve disciples (classmates) and with them, did change the world. At least three of them had nicknames. James and John, brothers with short fuses, got the moniker, Sons of Thunder. And then Simon Peter got the nickname Rock. Guess who gave it to him? Jesus. Jesus said of Simon Peter, "You shall be called Rock, and upon this rock, I will build my church" (Matthew 16:18).

Our Catholic friends understand that passage to mean that Peter was the first Pope. Most Protestants would take it to mean that upon the profession of faith in Christ that Peter had just made, upon that kind of profession, Christ built his church. Regardless of who has the correct interpretation, one thing is sure; Simon Peter must have been one strong dude to get such a nickname from Jesus.

I would give anything if someone had nicknamed me Rock. Wormy is about as opposite of Rock as one could get. Rock symbolizes strength. Wormy symbolizes weakness. Simon Peter had to be strong in his faith to endure the hardships that being a disciple would bring him. Tradition says that he was put to death by crucifixion for Christ. He literally took up his cross and followed Jesus. He was a rock.

I wonder what nickname my kids would give me. I hope it would be a strong, not weak, one. Kids everywhere need mentors and role models. So, be a rock, not a worm.

The Drama of the Paranoid Parent

I swear that the paranoids are out to get me. Maybe I watch too much news or read too many newspapers. Natalie and I were en route to her first ever college football game. It was a father/daughter weekend, and we had stopped at a McDonalds on Friday afternoon on the way to the game. We were headed to Alabama, and yes, we got our shots when we crossed the state line. McDonalds is where the drama unfolded—the drama of the paranoid parent.

He was sitting by himself, drinking a Coke. He was middle-aged with not much hair, and he smiled as we made eye contact. He then smiled at my six-year-old. That's when I said to myself, "He looks just like one of those pictures on the FBI's list of Most Wanted." I had good reason to be paranoid. After all, he was sitting by himself and he smiled at my kid. That's enough, right? And he looked like what I imagined The Boston Strangler would have looked like.

I had stopped at McDonalds for a bathroom break for me, not her (that was a shocker). I started to tell her to wait for me, "I'll be right out." That's when paranoia jumped all over me, like tattoos on Dennis Rodman. I thought, "I'm going to come out of this restroom, and she will be gone." After all, he looked like a "dirty old man." What to do? That's when Natalie said, much to my relief, "I'll play on the playground." There were several kids and parents there, and as far as I could tell, none of them resembled Al Capone. And so she played safely.

As I came out of the restroom, a young lady exited the ladies room next to me. She was obviously, based on what she was wearing, a high school band majorette. She had on the uniform. She was an attractive, blonde, maybe 16 or 17-years-old. And guess what? Darn, if she didn't go and sit at the table with the "dirty old man." And I watched as they talked and laughed. She left and they hugged, and I felt like such a fool—big, fat paranoid fool. The "dirty old man" was apparently a loving father, who I am guessing, met his daughter every Friday before the game at McDonalds to share a Coke and to wish her "good luck." They had a father/daughter outing before a football game, just like I was having with mine. And I wonder what he thought about me?

I had made him out, in my mind, to be a monster. I had prejudged him in the worst way, based on what? How he looked? His smile? Because he reminded me of a picture on a poster? Because he was a man sitting by himself? I was embarrassed and grateful that he couldn't read my mind.

I know we aren't supposed to be prejudiced—that is to pre-judge others. "Judge not others, and you will not be judged" (Matthew 7:1). But we do it a lot, don't we? I know I do. I really have to battle not to judge someone on the basis of the clothes they wear or the color of their skin. If there is a test given, I failed it at McDonalds.

I've got to quit watching "America's Most Wanted." Too much of that will ruin your father/daughter weekend and your Big Mac.

Field Peas

I have to admit, it was pretty impressive. I'm not bragging, but people at the pot luck dinner were impressed. What impressed people at the pot luck dinner is that I walked into the kitchen, surveying the food as I am apt to do, and I pointed to some peas in a dish and said, "Those peas are from Dothan, Alabama." Well, that wasn't the impressive part. The impressive part was when the lady who brought the peas said, "Yes, I got them in Dothan." I'm not saying that anybody's jaw dropped or that I started signing autographs, but you have to admit you can't do that. You can't walk into a kitchen and point at the okra and say, "That's from Savannah," and be right about it.

Okay, how did I know that the peas were from Dothan, apart from my normal prophetic, ministerial, soothsayer abilities? Truth is, I've eaten those peas all my life, having grown up in Dothan, and I have never eaten them anywhere else. I don't know if they are not grown anywhere else, but I know them when I see them. And they just happen to be the best peas on the planet.

And I thought I would never eat them again. You see, since Dad died in '03, and my older brother, who also lived in Dothan, died in '06, and since Mom moved a year ago, I have no one left there. The only occasion I have to go to Dothan is for a class reunion or to visit the cemetery. And so, I thought I had eaten my last, grown in Dothan dirt, field peas. May we have a moment of silence?

Eating Dothan field peas took me on a journey in my mind, though a brief one, back home. It reminded me of all the Thanksgiving meals that Mom cooked and how Dad and my older brother loved those peas. The journey took me back to Turkey Day football games in the front yard and to times of playing golf with Dad and my brothers. For a brief moment, eating peas made me a child again. It made me thankful that the person I am today is in large part a result of the experiences I had as a kid in Dothan. Field peas may have nourished my body, but good parents, fine brothers, an excellent church, and faithful friends nourished the soul. As one writer put it, "Who you are is who you were." We are products to some degree, for better or worse, of our environment and the people and things that nourished us.

Of course, we don't want to dwell too much on that. If we dwell too much in the past then the past becomes an excuse for what we have not become. We also should move off of the past because we have all changed so much. Who I am now is a lot different than who I was as a kid. I certainly don't look the same, having consumed too many hamburgers and not enough peas. I am not the same because I have matured emotionally and spiritually from the kid who played football in the front yard. I'm a grown-up now, and I know that Paul was right, "When I was a child, I spoke like a child, I thought like a child, I reasoned like a child; when I became an adult, I put an end to childish ways" (1 Corinthians 13:11).

So, invite me over, and I will take a stab at where the okra was grown. And I will tell you some stories about a little boy who loved field peas.

From "Wassup?" to "Hi"

This time wasn't as bad. Last time, which was the first time, was awful. This time was the second time taking our son to college, having now begun his sophomore year. When you take that first child off for the freshman year, now that is something. We cried on the way home, and reminisced, and cried some more. There was a hole in our hearts the size of Donald Trump's ego. That time, the first time, we hugged, and then bid a tearful "goodbye." This time, the second time, it was a pat on the back and a "see ya."

Life and people change, and we learn to adjust. We should be glad to see our kids grow up and learn independence. Rites of passage they are called: learning to drive, first date, going off to college. We celebrate those special moments in their lives, though those moments can be really difficult for Mom and Dad to swallow.

There was another sign for us that our son has grown up. For years now, when you called his cell phone and got his voice mail, you got, "Wassup? This is Tyler. Leave a message." I never really cared for "wassup," but I didn't lodge a formal complaint. I figured that was his business, not mine. Well, this summer he had a real job working in a law firm, and I noticed that his voice mail changed from "Wassup?" to "Hi, you have reached..." I thought I had dialed the wrong number. These are subtle signs that our kids have passed into the next phase of life.

Someone said that "raising a child is the process of losing a child." Some of these rights of passage hurt. Sending a kid off to college hurts. I haven't had the experience of marrying off my daughter, but I can only imagine. But it is a good kind of hurt, because it is mingled with joy over their maturity and happiness.

Every "hello" that we have in life, has tucked away in the back pocket, a "goodbye." The "hello" of the birth of our children has the "goodbye" of putting them on a school bus or moving them into a college dorm room. Sure it hurts, but it's what you want for them. You want them to go out on their own and make their own way. But it hurts because we love them so much.

Some folk shy away from having deep relationships (or any for that matter) because they fear the goodbye. But what we must do is to keep nurturing all our relationships and not shy away from loving. Fear of the painful goodbye will paralyze us if we let it. In the words of author Charles Poole, "It is better to know the pain of saying a goodbye that hurts than never to know the joy of saying a hello that matters." Then he adds, "To steel yourself against ever having to say a goodbye that hurts is to steal yourself, to rob your joy, and to diminish your life."[6]

---

[6] Charles E. Poole, *The Tug of Home* (Macon: Peake Road, 1997) 81.

And who wants their kids to go through life always saying "Wassup?" Not me.

"For everything there is a season, and a time for every matter under heaven" (Ecclesiastes 3:1).

Sweet Dreams

I did what I have often done. I listened as Natalie read her book before bed. We said a prayer and then talked for a minute. On this particular night I said something to the effect, "I love you, and if you ever have any problems, please tell me." "No, I'm fine," she said.

Next night, same thing. Only this time she said, "I do have a problem." My heart sank past my arthritic knee to my ankles. "What is it?" "I've had some bad dreams," she said. You see, some of our friends have had their house broken into twice, and Natalie has had some bad dreams about that. I reassured her that we are safe, the doors are locked, etc. I told her that almost all break-ins happen during the day when no one is home. She then reminded me that those same friends also discovered someone in the bushes outside their home—at night. I could quickly tell that I was losing that argument, so I figured the best I could do was to give her a hug and try to make her feel secure.

A few weeks later, same routine. Only this time, it was the night before her class at school was having ice cream as an end of the year party. I said, "How about some sweet dreams about ice cream?" The next morning, sure enough, "What did you dream about?" "Ice cream with sprinkles," she said, with a smile.

What would you rather your kid dream about—break-ins or Blue Bell? It pained me to think that she was worried, as an eight-year-old, about break-ins. She is too young and innocent to have to worry about such stuff. I also worried that I had not been reassuring enough to her about our home security. I think she knows that none of us are, and no home is, completely safe.

We parents often live with the illusion that we can keep our kids totally safe and that we are in complete control. Try as we might, we can't protect our kids from everything. An angry tornado in the South reminds us that no home is completely immune from the forces of nature. No amount of hand sanitizer can protect our little ones from germs and viruses that we can't even see. I'm pretty good at fighting things I can see, but that invisible stuff is hard to fight. We also can't protect our kids from hurt, whether a skinned knee or a bruised ego from the playground.

Maybe we need to let go of them and let them live. And let's have a little faith. Faith doesn't mean that bad stuff (like tornados and break-ins) won't happen. Faith just means that you have chosen to live a certain way and, with God's help, to deal with what comes your way.

"All things work together for good, to those who love God..." (Romans 8:28). Paul doesn't say that all things are good. He says that all things (good or bad) work together for good. That's where the faith comes in.

So, I'm hoping that my kid has lots more dreams about Blue Bell than break-ins—and with sprinkles on top.

Getting Punk'd by Your Kid

They got me good—they being my wife and nine-year-old daughter. I don't give much thought to April Fools' Day, and I haven't been "had" on that day in quite some time. But, this past April 1, I got punk'd by Natalie and Sheri. Getting punk'd is based on a TV reality show by that same name in which hidden camera practical jokes are played on unsuspecting folk—like me.

We take two cars to church because we go at different times. (I proudly say that we have never had an argument on the way to church.) That Sunday (April 1) we had taken two cars to the restaurant for lunch. As I waited for them inside the restaurant, Natalie came in and said she needed to borrow my keys because Mom had locked hers in her car in the parking lot. Nothing suspicious about that! So, I gave her my keys. That is when Natalie, as part of the April Fools' joke, took my house key off my key chain.

After lunch I went home, as Sheri and Natalie said they had some errands to run (liars!). They actually went to a friend's house and waited for my call. I went home and reached for my house key. I have lots of senior moments these days, and I felt sure this was another one. Surely my house key had not fallen off my key chain. Is that possible? It had to be here. I had it that morning when I left the house early. I looked and looked, sure that I was somehow overlooking it. I was not. I said several "dad gums." Could it have fallen off in my car or in the driveway? I retraced my steps, carefully checking my path. No key.

In frustration, I called Sheri's cell. Anticipating my call, she had her cell on speaker phone so as to broadcast my call over the neighborhood. "Sheri, I can't find my house key. It is the darnedest thing. How could it have fallen off my key chain? I used it this morning."

Then I heard enough laughter to make Jerry Seinfeld jealous. "April Fools," Sheri and Natalie giggled. And giggled. The friends laughed and laughed some more. Finally, when the laughter subsided, they decided to rescue me and bring my key home.

That's when I began plotting revenge. Later that evening I snuck upstairs with a cup of water and placed it on top of Natalie's partially opened door. I then went downstairs and waited with the anticipation of a race car in the starting gate at Indy. I waited for the "Oh my gosh, I'm drenched." I waited for the unwinding moment of revenge that would be so sweet. It never came. The water missed and got the carpet and not the kid.

Revenge is no joke. The Old Testament way of "an eye for an eye" or "tooth for a tooth," (lex talionis or practically known as "tit for tat") falls far short of Christian faith. Jesus taught His followers to "turn the other cheek," and "go the second mile," as a response to those who would harm us. Jesus articulated the principle of non-retaliation in personal relations. He even took it a huge step forward and taught His followers to "love your enemies and pray for those who persecute you" (Matthew 5: 44).

I get what He is saying, but Natalie and Sheri had better watch out next year. You know the old saying: "a punk'd for a punk'd."

So, Take a Lot of Pictures

Was it worth it? Time will tell, but I'm guessing it was. Was the expense for the Daddy/Daughter Dance worth it? I don't even want to know a grand total, because knowing it might cause cardiac arrest. I do know that the grand total includes $30 to register, a new dress with matching new shoes, a hair appointment, wrist corsage, dinner before the dance, and pictures at the dance. I am afraid to total that up knowing that it might rival the annual budget of a third world country.

But was it worth it? The "Was it worth it?" question could be answered by the "Did you have a good time?" question. So, did I have a good time? Sure, spending three or so hours with Natalie and watching her excitement is a good time for me. But I didn't dance one dance. The reason I didn't dance one dance is because a Baptist preacher with a bad knee is a joke on the dance floor. So, I got to sit this one out, much to Natalie's delight. She danced with friends. I sat on the sideline with my crutch and overindulged in the chocolate fountain.

But what I did get out of it, besides a good time with my daughter, were some good memories and pictures. Since we have now been to several of these dances (and have several more to go), the memories of one might fade into the others. Daddy/Daughter Dances are pretty much the same each year except that one year she wears a red dress or blue dress, or this year an orange one. With time, I will simply remember the Daddy/Daughter Dances as fun events with my daughter, but one will not stand out from the others (except this is the crutch year).

But what will stand out is the picture. Each year I buy the picture package which includes several wallet size and one 8x10, which we have framed. We now have several of these framed pictures, and I cherish each one. It is the 8x10 that will be the lasting memory for me. When I am 80 (and broke from these dances) at least I will have several wonderful pictures as memories of special nights. The nursing home won't be so lonely because of these 8x10s.

"What is your life? For you are a mist that appears for a little while and then vanishes" (James 4:14).

So, take a lot of pictures.

Duct Tape

Many of the guys wore duct tape on their shoes. No, this is not some new fashion statement (duct tape now comes in many different colors), like wearing your pants down around your knees. And, by the way, the guys wearing the duct tape on their shoes just happened to be in a funeral. Say what? Yea, you read it right. A bunch of guys wore suits and duct tape. Why, pray tell, why? Well, they did it to honor their deceased loved one, Mr. Art Cole. You see, Mr. Cole wasn't really enamored with fashion, and so when his shoes started to fall apart, he would just put some duct tape on them. He found it to be a quick, inexpensive fix. So some of the guys in his family, to honor his memory, wore duct tape on their wing tips. I thought it was a neat way to remember Art.

How will you be remembered? Or better yet, what are you doing that your loved ones will remember? Mr. Art Cole's family has some great memories of him (many more than duct tape) because he spent time with them, and he did things that they will remember. He fished with them. He told them stories (Art never let the truth get in the way of a good story). If you don't spend time with your family or give them something to remember, then guess what? They won't remember things that didn't happen. They won't remember you taking them fishing if you never take them fishing. They won't remember stories you never told them.

My two children have never, I mean never, climbed into my lap and said, "Dad, tell me another one of your sermons." But time and time again, they have said, "Tell me a story about when you were a little boy." And so I have told them about the time Shane, the big dog next door, ran me up a tree. And they have heard the story (they love this one) about the time my best growing up friend, Sly, rode his new bike into a tree. But if I don't tell them, they won't remember.

I wonder how many kids walk away from their dad's funeral wondering if dad was proud of them. "He told me he loved me, but he never told me he was proud of me," some children say. Kids won't remember things you don't say. So, if you are proud of your kids, put down this book and go and tell them right now. What are you waiting for?

The late Erma Bombeck wrote a column "Time through the Eyes of a Child." One of the paragraphs in it went like this: "When I was young, Daddy was going to come to school and watch me in a play. I was the fourth Wise Man, just in case one of the other three got sick, but he had an appointment, and it took longer than he thought…so there wasn't time."

Duct tape is used to cover up a lot of flaws, tears, and irregularities. Art had some in his shoes and, I guess, in his soul. We all do. But with Art, duct tape revealed more than it covered. Duct tape revealed that he wasn't too concerned with how he dressed or how he looked. He had more important things to worry about. That's not a bad lesson to pass on to your kids and their kids. So, how will you be remembered?

Index

CPSIA information can be obtained at www.ICGtesting.com
Printed in the USA
LVOW10s0254121113

360959LV00002B/3/P

9 781938 230554